AURAS

Interpretation
&
Comprehension

Dictation from The Great White Brotherhood

Bob Sanders

DISCLAIMERS

This is a free eBook. You are free to give it away (in unmodified form) to whomever you wish. If you have paid for this eBook you should request or seek an immediate refund.

The author has made every effort to ensure the accuracy of the information within this book was correct at time of publication. The author does not assume and hereby disclaims any liability to any party for any loss, damage, or disruption caused by errors or omissions, whether such errors or omissions result from accident, negligence, or any other cause.

COPYRIGHT

PREFACE

The art of developing along the spiritual path has been considered by many a long and difficult road involving much meditation and performing breathing exercises and possibly contortions of the body as if all these exercises in some way would force an opening into the spiritual realms above and beyond any natural means of communicating with the God spheres.
We see yogis able to perform the most outlandish contortions of their bodies, developed over many years and amazing their chelas or students who sweat and strain to copy the contortions of the master.

It should be obvious to any student of esoteric science that any technique that is not relevant to all people in all dimensions must have a flaw somewhere, for spiritual development is carried out in areas far removed from the physical planes of Earth.
Thus, any technique that would have no meaning outside of physicality must be meaningless.
We are interested in uncovering the secret path to perfection that we may continue to use long after we quit the Earth plane, thus the aim of this book is to reveal to all students of esoteric development, techniques that he may use both during his incarnation and on into the spiritual realms so that a continuous and coherent pattern of development may be developed not requiring a physical body and not requiring the student to waste precious time in developing contortion acts designed principally to impress gullible people.
The path to God is based on truth, honesty and simplicity, not contortions of the physical body that would have no relevance once physical incarnation is finished.
We intend in this book to introduce to all who are willing to learn sufficient concerning the auras and their relevance to man both incarnate and in spiritual form, so that a complete understanding of the astral dimensions, with all their ramifications, so that the student will be fully armed should he enter them and to do so safely.

We intend also to describe the beings that are found in these dimensions and how to interact with them both safely and correctly.
Finally, we hope to explain why auras exist and how we can navigate through them in an adult fashion as we explore the realms that God has created for our pleasure and education.

This will be a book largely concentrating on the auras and it is hoped that, at the end of this book, the student will have complete knowledge of how the, up till now, largely hidden information regarding the higher aspects of life will be fully understood.

CHAPTER 1

HOW DID IT ALL START?

In the beginning, as we have explained in the previous books, God created 8 frequencies or carrier waves as a means of expressing in as concrete a fashion as possible his curiosity of how life in general and man in particular would react in these frequencies. We wish to explain that any life, on any particular frequency, vibrates in harmony with that frequency.

However, God himself being made of a vibration that we term light, thought it is a good idea not only that living entities should vibrate to the frequency of any carrier wave but, to allow independent movement within that frequency to denote those creatures with independent variations of that frequency.

Thus, each and every being or object on any plane not only vibrates in harmony with the frequency of that plane, but each entity or object also vibrates to a slightly, independent variation of that frequency.

Thus, if we could see with sufficient clarity those beings or objects within any carrier wave, we would notice that everything would shine with the basic color of that frequency, but each and every object would shine a slightly different aspect of that frequency.

This may be a little difficult to understand that for instance, if the quiescent color was blue, each and every object would also glow blue but there would be slight variants to that blue color so that everything within that base blue color could be seen as an individual aspect of that blue color.

So, if we can explain in a slightly different way, all the beings and objects within the blue carrier wave would themselves glow with a blue light but, individually, the color blue would be modified slightly for all things so that each and every object within that blue carrier wave could and would stand out distinctly from the basic blue carrier wave.

We wish to explain also, as some artists will already know, a color, blue in this example is actually made from blending a variety of colors and that there is no such thing as a single vibration that we could call blue.

All variants of the color blue are a mixture of other colors blended together to create a color referred to as blue, although it might be a dark, midnight blue, a bright "forget me not blue", a sky blue up to the palest blue imaginable. Yet we refer to all these variations as blue.

As is so often the case we were using the color blue as an example.

In fact, the basic carrier waves created by God do not have any color ascribed to them any more than the carrier waves of TV channels have color.

We described the carrier waves as having color in an attempt to describe to you that each carrier wave has a unique frequency, but that all the beings and objects within that particular carrier wave has slight variations of that unique carrier wave.

The reason we did this is because on Earth, using conventional physics, if, for example, there was a carrier wave of, say, 1 million cycles per second (1 MHz), to put other frequencies within it would alter the quiescent frequency of 1MHz and it would no longer be that frequency any longer.

But, in a similar way that broadcast stations send out a program on a particular carrier wave and encode within it information on different frequencies that we perceive as sound or vision, so all things on a particular astral carrier wave are slight variations of that carrier wave and thus do not blend with the carrier wave.

We should also mention for those that understand how broadcasting or telephones work, in those circumstances the carrier wave is vastly different in frequency, so the sound and vision broadcasted within that carrier wave can be separated from the carrier wave by simply eliminating that carrier wave.

But, in the case of God's setup – if we may use that familiar expression – the quiescent vibration and the independent vibrations of those things found on that particular vibration, or carrier wave, are slight indeed.

So, they are in part an aspect of that carrier wave and at the same time independent from it.

Higher physics permits this apparently impossible effect of being blended within a carrier wave and at the same time separate from it.

This effect of being part of a carrier wave but of being unique within it is important to understand, as it is this effect that enables us to have dimensions to travel within whilst having a unique identity.

Thus, it is that we can, thanks to being total carrier waves and yet unique within them that gives the ability to all be one and yet all be independent entities at the same time.

So, we have arrived at the point where God created 8 carrier waves and put life of all sorts upon these carrier waves and yet denoted each life object a unique aspect, no matter what it was and is, to consider itself an independent object.

We wish to repeat for any that have not read the previous books that God, being the creator of all life, gave a life force to everything that has been created by the servants of God.

Thus sand, water, planets, plants, animals, man, galaxies, space is all alive and is all both one and the same, yet independent aspects of life.

As we have mentioned before, this is not an easy concept to comprehend and it can only really be appreciated when one develops a certain degree of spiritual awareness.

Yet it is a great truth to realize that all that exists in any form, any dimension, is one and yet individual aspects of that oneness at the same time.

But, let us progress.

We have described in the book "The Path Of Mankind" how God created all that he put on the high dimensions, including principally man, so we will not mention it all here.

Sufficient to remind you that to understand this book as it progresses it is important to have a clear understanding of the first few chapters of the aforementioned book.

So, we need now to explore what came after God created the 8 carrier waves and put man on the first two of them.

As we have already said, God put a lot more than just man on these two carrier waves but our interest being primarily that of investigating man we will largely ignore the rest of life contained within those two carrier waves.

It might be questioned why God only put man on the first two carrier waves, 8 & 7, but we hope that as the book progresses understanding will be revealed.

Thus, it must be appreciated that if man was only placed, initially on frequencies 8 & 7, the other 6 frequencies were sterile, just being frequencies each of different vibrations but devoid of life.

God waited patiently as man developed on the higher two frequencies through being presented with a variety of "problems", for want of a better word, and thus, eventually, became sufficiently aware of the complexities of life to be taken to the next level (the next step) that God had already created in thought form in his mind.

This step was to create a plane where imagination could be developed.

God realized soon after he created life that it would not be enough to be a carbon copy of himself nor would it be useful to create everyone the same like robots.

So, the decision was taken to introduce imagination into the minds of men.

We will also say that the concept of imagination was also, at the same time introduced into the "mind" of all things: animals, vegetable, mineral, liquid, gas and so on, with greater or lesser success.

But we concentrate principally on man.

Imagination was created on the 6th plane of creation.

CHAPTER 2

THIS IMAGINARY WORLD

Thus, we need to investigate this 6th plane and analyse what goes on there and how it contributes to the creation of imagination within all things including man.

Everything is created from vibration. Everything is actually created from light -star light - that can be varied by the Archangels that work directly for the God force because, God, being the prime creator of all that exists in all dimensions, does not participate directly in any aspect of creation. God, having created all that exists waits for the results of his efforts to return so that he can expand in wisdom. These Archangels could not possibly be imagined by man but they do, indeed, exist and manipulate the whole galaxy, and many more galaxies outside of the aegis of man's knowledge, keeping everything in balance according to God's prime directive.

So, these Archangels are responsible for creating and maintaining everything everywhere. They are able to do this because everything is vibration – frequency - thus by varying the frequency of something they are able to keep all in balance.

If we may try to explain this in a more down to Earth fashion, imagine a group of technicians sitting in front of a large panel connected to a mass of dials and each technician constantly manipulating the dials as a situation altered and required adjustment by all other dials, each dial attached to a frequency generator. Thus, these technicians constantly scanning various meters and warning devices, adjusting frequencies so that all remained in equilibrium.

This oversimplification has, of course, no relevance when we are considering the work of the Archangels but, if it gives a small insight into what really goes on in the multiverse, it will have served its purpose.

Having given a brief overview of the Archangels that control the universe, let us hone in on the 6th dimension and try to understand more of what happens here.
We have stated that the 6th dimension is where imagination is housed.
But what is imagination and why should it be housed on such a high vibration, for the 6th plane is, indeed, high in terms of spiritual development? It is the house of genius.

Now we must return to these Archangels and how they reacted when they realized that the prime directive of God was to create wisdom everywhere and to return that wisdom to God so that newer creations could be endowed with some of that wisdom.

The Archangels considered creations that existed in the higher two dimensions (7th and 8th) and examined closely the way that they reacted to various problems that had been presented to them and they realized that these early versions of man had to learn everything by actual experience. They had, to use an understandable expression, to burn their fingers before they realized that heat burned and hurt.

In other words, these early men lacked the ability to 'imagine'.
The Archangels, who themselves being vastly superior to any person incarnate or disincarnate had themselves developed imagination long eons ago and actively used it in helping and controlling the various frequencies of light, enabling them to visualize the outcome of any manipulation before effecting it and thus, largely, avoiding mistakes, for mistakes on global scales would be catastrophic. Imagination enabled the Archangels from avoiding making such mistakes.

So, it occurred to these Archangels to create a frequency in one of the bands of carrier waves we call dimensions that would correspond to the frequency of imagination.

You may remember in chapter one we mentioned that a carrier wave could be a certain frequency - and in that example we chose the colour blue to use as an example - and we also said that a slight variation of that basic colour could be introduced and that it would, at the same time, be part of and also distinct from, the original Blue carrier wave.

Well, the Archangels looked at the frequency of the 6th carrier wave and were able to manipulate into that quiescent frequency a slight variation that, as we have explained before, became part of and distinct from the original frequency.

So, now we have the carrier wave and an empty variant rather like, for those who understand using computers, to create an empty file within the hard disc of the computer.

Into this file, they put imagination.
Let us describe how this was done.
Everything is vibration - frequency. So, although this may be hard to appreciate, every aspect of everything is vibration. Every thought, every emotion, every aspect of personality is vibration all resonating at a certain frequency.

Even these mysterious and wonderful Archangels are made of vibrations, all working together to create what we term an Archangel.
This is because all is light and light is vibration - frequency. God is light – star light - and as God created everything as a reflection of himself, he created everything from star light shining at different frequencies to create everything, even the dismal planet Earth.

So, imagination is a vibration:
The Archangels understood this and so they manipulated the quiescent frequency of the 6th plane until it corresponded to the frequency of imagination.

We wish to make it quite clear that the quiescent frequency of the 6th dimension remained as it was created but all the same time it contained the vibration frequency of imagination.

But imagination is not a physical concept nor is it a concept that could have any solidity in and astral sense.

It is a concept that exists as an idea.

Words do not exist in any readily understandable language that adequately describes something that can exist as a real quantity and yet, at the same time only exists as a concept.

There were languages in the past that contained words to describe such matters but these have largely died out thanks to the efforts of the Archons who went to great lengths to destroy languages that described spiritual matters.

Sanskrit is one of the few remaining languages that can describe these concepts but very few people are really versed in understanding Sanskrit.

It must also be said that modern man usually has no ability to appreciate that something can exist in a real fashion but that something is itself just a thought. We are told that thoughts are things but, unless those thoughts are translated into solid objects, thoughts are largely dismissed.

But, when we can realize that all is vibration and each and every thought exists as a vibration in any frequency into which it is projected, we can start to appreciate that thoughts, indeed, are things. Those things may be invisible to our eyes but they do exist and can influence anyone who opens themselves to those thoughts.

Thus, thoughts can and do influence others.

Therefore, we hope that you can understand that by placing a vibration that corresponds to the frequency of the imagination, this 6th plane was now endowed with that attribute. The Archangels who already had developed imagination were able to isolate the frequency that corresponds to imagination and develop a pocket of vibration within the 6th carrier wave and so imagination was now active within that carrier wave.

We wish to repeat for the sake of clarity that God, having created everything as a reflection of his creative design to obtain wisdom from all of his creations working together, made everything the same at heart. Thus, all things contain the 8 carrier waves that God created and so, in the 6th carrier wave that all things have associated with them now had imagination.

As one can 'imagine', it took early man a long time to realize that he had something called imagination connected to him as a fundamental part of his makeup and, indeed, there are still many people who seldom or never make use of it. How often do we hear people say that if they can't see or measure something for them it does not exist? And they say it with pride as if dismissing imagination was something to be proud of - having their feet firmly planted on the ground.

And yet imagination is a wonderful, God given tool.

Imagination has helped create much of what exists in the world today. If it was not for imagination much of what exists that offers so much to creature comforts would not exist.

So, it is strange that those who reject imagination as "pie in the sky" nevertheless make daily use of things that only exist thanks to imagination of those inventors who visualized the tools that we have around us and brought them into reality. By "tools", we of course refer to the million and one objects of all sorts that are part of daily life now and contribute to the help and comfort that we have.

So, we reiterate, the 6th plane is the plane, the dimension, of imagination and, as we all have that 6th plane associated with us, we can all reach into that plane, that dimension and make use of imagination.

But we must say that, as all is one, there is only one 6th plane and thus when we reach into it to use imagination, we're all reaching into this one, unique area and we all make use of this one concept "imagination".
This, obviously, needs some explanation as you see yourself as a separate human being, a separate creation from any other object or person so you feel that when you sit down to imagine something - the solution to a problem, an invention that you wish to make, the reparation of something - you are using an imaginary force unique to you. And yet we said that there was only one area that contained imagination and all life forces, all over the galaxy enter this one unique plane and make use of the one force that we call imagination.

Logic would dictate that all our thoughts would get jumbled up and, if we tried to imagine something we would, in return, get just anyone's imagined thoughts.
The answer, of course, is found in frequency - vibration. Each person incarnate on this 3D world known as planet Earth vibrates in harmony with the frequency with which planet Earth is vibrating. Also, the whole of our galaxy is vibrating to that same frequency that we refer to as a carrier wave.

But you and everything else vibrates to a slight variant of that quiescent frequency.
We mentioned this at the beginning of this chapter and we will mention it again as it is important to understand this point.
The 3D world you currently live on is vibrating at a particular frequency that we call a carrier wave. Everything visible on Earth and everything that you can see in the night sky - on and on - is vibrating to a certain frequency as is every atom that constitutes what we refer to as solidity.
Further, every thought, every feeling, every emotion is also made up of this same carrier wave.

This is why we can say that all is one. Everything, everywhere is vibrating to this unique frequency.

So, why are things not jumbled up into an untidy mess?
The answer has already been mentioned. Within that carrier wave the Archangels charged with looking after the apparently solid galaxy - this 3D one that you are on at the moment - endowed each and every object: animal, vegetable and mineral with a unique variant of that base frequency that we refer to as a dimension.
This enables you to have the feeling that you are different from anyone else or any other object. Further, as we hope you can now realize, not only are you - every atom of your

being - vibrating at a slightly different variant of the 3D's quiescent frequency, so each and every thought is vibrating at a different variant of your frequency.

We will state this again to make it absolutely explicit. You live in a galaxy that vibrates to a carrier wave of a particular frequency.

But, to give you the sensation that you are a unique being, you vibrate to a slightly different frequency to the 3D carrier wave.

Now this is the point we wish to drive home. Each and every thought you have, each and every emotion, feeling - call it what you will - also has a slight variant of the 3D's quiescent frequency.

You must understand that a thought has a frequency slightly different from the quiescent frequency of the carrier wave of the 3D world.

Then the next thought has a slightly different frequency, then the next thought and the next, endlessly on and on. Each and every thought that you create in your mind, each and every emotion, each and every word that you speak has a slight variation compared to any other thought or word that you created in your mind previously.

But each and everyone is connected to your frequency.

This is extremely difficult to comprehend and difficult for us to describe but for students of cosmic awareness it is important to realize this so we will try to explain it one more time.

Your galaxy vibrates to the frequency of your 3D carrier wave. You exist as an individual because you vibrate to a slight variant of the 3D carrier wave.

Every thought, emotion, or spoken word is created as a unique slight variant of your particular variant of the carrier wave in which you live.

This last part is the most difficult to describe and comprehend.

Each and every thought that you had from your birth to the moment of your demise on your carrier wave has a unique frequency that separates it from any other thought, emotion or spoken word that you have had or will have. But they are all connected to your frequency and are part of you.

This applies, of course, to all humans, all animals, and all sentient things in the 3D galaxy.

Who can imagine that everything is constantly pouring out a stream of thoughts and each thought is encoded by a slightly different version of the entity thinking those thoughts. Each thought also encoded as a unique vibration slightly different from any previous thought or thought to come afterwards.

Further, to make it even more difficult to comprehend, all these thoughts, all these vibrations, not only of the thoughts we described above but the vibrations of all things that have existed, exist and will exist are all recorded in a sort of vast library that we term the Akashic Record.

Nothing is lost. Not any grain of sand that existed when the galaxy was created, up to each and every being: animal, vegetable, mineral, every single thought, word, emotion etc, has all been recorded for all time.

Thus, could the master Jesus say that the hairs on the head are numbered and not a single sparrow can fall to the ground without your father (God) knowing it.

This was what he was referring to. Everything is recorded.

Now you may be wondering what all the above has to do with the 6th plane, the plane of imagination?

The answer lies in the way the mind works.

We mentioned that everything is a vibration and, if this is true then imagination must also be a vibration.

But, if a thought goes out from someone into the dimension that contains imagination it is essential that this thought be separated from anyone else's thoughts because, as we also mentioned, there is only one dimension for all beings and so all thoughts sent to that plane or dimension need to be separated from every other being's thoughts going into the same area.

We hope that it should be obvious by now that each thought has its own frequency and so there can be any number of thoughts swirling into the 6th dimension but they are kept totally separated from each other because of this unique frequency that all things are encoded with.

We wish, also to express as clearly as we can that we are not only referring to living things on the Earth plane but also every entity living in the other astral planes anywhere in the multiverse: those living in the heavenly spheres and those we consider to be aliens and so on.

Any and all living entities throughout the entire universe created by God use this one dimension to send thoughts and to get answers from.

Now, this also enables a mysterious effect to take place by those who have trained their minds and this effect is that it is possible to tap into another person's thoughts and to share those thoughts.

This ability to share other's thoughts is what we call telepathy or channeling.

Telepathy is the ability of one person to send his thoughts into the 6th plane or dimension and to share his thoughts with someone else who is also sending his thoughts into that dimension.

This normally should not happen, of course, because each person's thoughts are encoded with the unique frequency exclusive to that person or to that creature or entity capable of that thought.

But it is possible, under a certain, special circumstance for two people to harmonize their frequency so that they are operating on the same frequency and thus can exchange thoughts.

Not everyone can do this, of course, because it takes much training to be able to alter the unique frequency of their encoded thoughts so that communication between two people can occur.

It is not the case of one person altering his frequency to match the frequency of another person.

What happens is that, though the desire of two people to communicate together, a third frequency is generated so that this communication can take place.

The 6th dimension - that of imagination - is where this communication takes place.

The fact that this occurs on the 6th plane also implies that both people must have reached that high state of spiritual awareness or it would be impossible for such communication to take place. Not everyone who desires to learn telepathy can do so unless and until they have reached the level of spiritual awareness to reach, consciously, into that area.

Having said that, all people, regardless of their level of spirituality development can send their thoughts into the 6th dimension and receive their personal, encoded, answer to their uniquely coded thoughts sent out but, to alter their frequencies to a different frequency so that someone else can do the same requires a conscious act on behalf of both parties to create a third unique frequency and is a difficult act requiring much training by both people.

This also implies that when the communication is finished each person returns to his own frequency and the joint communication stops until both parties decide to communicate again. Thus, are everyone's normal thoughts kept private to each other.

How is it that one person can alert another person that he wishes to communicate with that person?
As we mentioned, the way telepathy works is by two people creating a third unique frequency that is shared, jointly, by both people.
So, each such person carries with him two frequencies. The first is that person's uniquely encoded thought process that is exclusive to him but, at the same time he has associated with him his second, modified, vibration or frequency that is normally not used in day to day thoughts. But it is there, within the consciousness of both people even when it is not being used.
So, if one person wishes to communicate with the other person, he switches off his first frequency related to thoughts and switches over to the second frequency. Then he sends out the thought, the desire to the other person that he wishes to communicate with him.
If the second person does not have his mind particularly occupied with thoughts, that person's second frequency picks up the communication desire of the first person and the second person is alerted to the fact that the first person wishes to communicate with him. Then he stills completely his first frequency and uses his modified frequency to "talk" to the first person.

This, of course, is the way that these books are produced. The person incarnate has been trained to modify his normal thought frequency to match a similar thought frequency of a person in the heavenly spheres and so information can flow from the mind of the person in the higher sphere, into the 6th dimension, is picked up by the thought process of the incarnate person and so the information flows.
Hopefully, if both parties can still their normal thought related frequencies so that only the modified frequencies are used, the information will flow accurately.
Should either one of the two people lose that focus on the modified frequency and switch back to his normal thought frequency then, of course, the communication is lost until one

of the two people realize the error they have made and switches back to the modified frequency and then the information can flow again.

This switching back and forth between the two frequencies is a frequent source of error made by those desirous of channeling.

Thus, it is that, if someone is using their normal frequency to hear a voice speaking to them, ignoring the possibility of influence by external, malevolent forces, fortunately very rare, the voice that the recipient hears is coming straight from their imagination because the imagination is always at work trying to send us sound and vision (voice and image). The problem is further exacerbated by the fact that, often the voice that the channeller hears sounds very similar to the normal voice that the person hears when he is thinking so it is almost impossible for many people to differentiate between his mind's voice speaking to him via the plane of imagination and the voice of a guide trying to communicate with the person.

So, for correct and accurate transfer of information to take place between any two people, both parties must have learned to still their normal mind.

However, the ability to still the mind is a hard - fought battle and few have the patience to fight with the mind until it cedes to the desire of the chela and that chela can at last sit in silence, master of his thoughts, or rather master of his ability to control his thoughts.

Thus, it is that many people, some well known and respected spent their lives writing books, giving lectures and acquiring large followings but the information being disseminated was, in fact, coming from their minds and not from a higher source.

It is the quality of the information that denotes the difference.

Those wishing to advance in cosmic wisdom would do well to be careful to whom they listen.

It is difficult for the novice to differentiate between information coming from any two people.

It is possible, occasionally, to get clues from the fact that the person who is quoting from his own imagination plane might well have a well stocked library of reference books from which he gleans his information and attends conferences on his chosen subject, making notes or obtaining recordings of the various speakers so that, privately, he can prepare his books and speeches using his own mind and not that of a high source. This is dishonest if deliberately done and the person who commits that sin of lying - for that is what it is - will pay for that sin when his incarnation finishes and he returns to heaven.

We are referring, of course, to those "teachers" who go into a sort of trance, or pretend to, and pretend also to be in communication with a spirit source who disseminates his "wisdom" to an audience that cling to his every word. Thus, if the teacher, medium, or whatever he calls himself, is dishonest, that so called medium is aware that he is just quoting from books and other sources that he has previously carefully prepared.

There are others, of course, that think that they are truly in touch with external sources of wisdom and give talks that, once again, are just coming from their own minds. This is not dishonest but, once the medium has exhausted his meager knowledge of cosmic wisdom either repeats it in talk after talk and just fills his talks with meaningless platitudes.

Once again it is up to the student to be careful to whom he listens.

A true medium needs no library, attends no conferences, and, indeed, goes to great lengths to avoid filling his mind with publications coming from others.
The job of a true medium is just to act as a channel, a conduit between a source of cosmic wisdom and the audience.
The medium requires no education on the subjects being discussed. His task is to make contact with the source of higher knowledge, clear his mind, and let the information flow.
He requires no adoration from the public for the wisdom he disseminates because he is fully aware that he has little wisdom himself. The wisdom is coming from an external source, and he is just the conduit allowing that information to be published in one form or another. He takes no credit for the information disseminated but he deserves thanks for all the hard work he puts into learning telepathy and for the time and energy it takes to receive information such as is being given in these various books and talks we are privileged to share with you.

So, we have spent considerable amount of time to explain how the 6th plane, that of imagination, is used in telepathic communication because that, "skill", if we can thus describe it is latent with all people and, in the future, man will use telepathy to replace the telephone systems that are so popular at the moment.
This will be a good thing because the evil forces are capable of putting within the carrier waves that bring telephonic communication, certain other frequencies that are nefarious to all life.
Once telepathy becomes the universal means of communication, the telephone systems will be switched off and thus these dangerous frequencies will cease to be broadcast.

We mentioned previously that to create a telepathic communication between two people it was necessary for both parties to modify their quiescent vibration to create a third that both parties shared.
It will be appreciated, we hope, that this third frequency is unique to just the two people desirous of communicating telepathically and thus is private, exclusive, to the two people.
But, the destiny of mankind is, one day, to be able to communicate with many people much as is done today using telephones.

Just as we have an agenda, a list of all our friends, relations, business partners, and so on with whom we communicate telephonically, we need a method of doing the same by telepathy.
Now, if we can continue for a moment to use the concept of telephones, each one of the people with whom we communicate we do so by sharing our telephone numbers. This gives us an exclusive connection between the two people. Once the communication finished we cut the connection and that gives both parties the opportunity to make fresh calls to other people.
So, we dial another number, only we do not use dials any more but just buttons.
To communicate telepathically with a variety of people we need a similar system.

So, we return to the system that we mentioned previously where we stated that two people could not exactly share their personal frequencies but created a third one by common agreement between the two people that enable them to share thoughts.

This concept can be taken on indefinitely. We can, with someone else, create a third frequency, exclusive to these two people so that a private communication can be carried on.

This, for the person whom we were considering earlier means that he would now have three frequencies available to him. First his basic frequency that gives him his sense of identity as a unique individual. Then a second frequency with which he was able to communicate telepathically with a person who had that frequency. Now we are adding a third frequency by which he can contact yet another person with whom he shares his third frequency.

This technique of creating more and more slightly different frequencies, each one exclusively designed to communicate with an individual on a private basis can be carried on endlessly in a very similar fashion to someone having a large list of telephone numbers, each one of which gives him private access to that person.

But this idea can be expanded to a group communication. It is possible for a group of people to share a frequency, rather like it is possible to share telephone numbers in order to create what is termed a conference.

Telepathy, providing two people have created a common frequency, is limitless. It is not affected by distance nor by different dimensions.

It is the natural way that mankind was intended to communicate and is destined to return.

Telepathy was discouraged by our arch enemies the Archons, because above the simple fact of being able to share thoughts with someone it is also a means of sharing truth about what the person is thinking.

With a normal conversation or a telephonic communication most people are just limited to listening to the words our correspondent is saying and any other thoughts, any other agenda that one or both of the parties might have, remains hidden.

But with telepathy we can, if we wish, delve behind the spoken thoughts being transmitted and find the words, the thoughts that are not being spoken. Now, polite people would not do this. They would not delve into the private thoughts that the correspondent does not wish to share, but it is a technique that is useful to uncover any negative intentions someone might have.

As one party is speaking, the second party listening is not only able to capture the words being spoken but is able to capture, also, the hidden thoughts.

This is because when using telepathy, we do not speak aloud, we think with our mind what we wish to say and if we have a hidden agenda entwined with the words that we wish to convey - the thoughts that we hope the recipient will hear in his mind as words - inevitably are contained the negative thoughts. Thus, the person transmitting his thoughts has to choose his thoughts carefully, selecting from the mass of negative thoughts in his mind, just the ones that he hopes will sound positive and he hopes that all the negative thoughts will not be picked up by the recipient of the thoughts.

But it is quite easy when using telepathy for the person listening to the selected thoughts, to reach a little deeper into the mind of the first person and then his true thoughts are transmitted.

If these deep thoughts are of peace and love, there is no problem, but if behind thoughts of peace and love there are actual thoughts of war, conflict, hatred, and so on, this is bad news for the person sending his thoughts for his true thoughts are revealed.

This, obviously, did not suit the Archons at all.

So, many thousands of years ago, shortly after the Extinction Level Event that destroyed Atlantis, as humanity slowly recovered and repopulated the Earth, it was a golden opportunity for the Archons to eliminate any means of communication except for the spoken word.

Of course, there were always those selected psychopaths that were inducted into the "mystery schools" that were taught the skill of world domination by evil reptilians who, themselves, were being influenced by the Archons and these reptilians taught those who were selected to rule, to use telepathy so that the public could not hear communications passing between these evil groups of people.

Anyone who discovered telepathy by chance was quickly removed.

So, we had a situation for a long time where only priests and rulers - all selected psychopaths - were taught telepathy and the general public had to use the spoken word.

We still see some evidence today of paintings on temple walls in Egypt of the reptilians teaching the chosen leaders of Egypt the skills required for domination of the people of that place and of that era.

However, times change and we are now in a time where it is once again the moment to start to introduce at least the concept of telepathy and how it works.

We are not yet, at the time of writing this book, totally free of Archon domination but that time will come and children will be taught telepathy amongst other esoteric skills.

But this time those skills will be used for good and not for evil.

So, having examined telepathy and how it has to pass from mind to mind via the 6th plane - using imagination - let us continue by studying how more mundane thoughts also pass by and through this extraordinary plane or dimension as it helps us to create thoughts and also to create the world in which we live regardless of which dimension we live in (or on depending on how one regards living in or on a vibrating carrier wave).

Thoughts start, surprisingly enough in a variety of areas of our spiritual concept. No thoughts, let us make it plain, start in the brain or even in the mind.

The brain is a flesh and blood organism that enables the body to operate. That is all.

The mind, which can be considered to be the spiritual version of the brain does a little more than the brain in that it not only helps the physical brain by telling it which parts of the body to keep working but also sends some basic emotions into the chakra points of the body. We will discuss the mind in greater detail at a later date.

But rest assured that, generally, thoughts have little or no connection with the mind and even less with the brain.

Thoughts, generally, are created in the higher self.

The higher self, for those who are not familiar with that term is considered to be the personal aspect of God.

This is true but is a simplification of how the God force works and how the spiritual construction of any object from a grain of sand to a human is constructed.

All things are immensely complex in construction and our task of explaining how life works is made very difficult because the vast amount of how life is put together, like a giant jigsaw puzzle, is totally unknown to man at the moment and, to explain how any one part works, requires an understanding of how all the rest works, for the God force that was used to construct life, works as a cohesive whole and not one piece could be removed or examined independently of the whole.

And yet we would not expect anyone to be able to grasp the whole without first understanding the separate parts.

We keep coming back to the chicken and egg conundrum.

How can we understand the whole without understanding the individual parts but how can we understand the parts if we need, first and at the same time to understand the whole?

So, all we can do is to explain using analogy.

We will at this point apologise in advance for some of the explanations that we will be forced to give because we realize that, for some people - perhaps many - we will lose you on route. This is not at all our desire and we go to great lengths to simplify complicated topics so that all can follow and thus grow in wisdom but, perforce, we must sometimes link what appears to be disparate elements together in our feeble attempts to explain life.

Now, where to begin our attempt to explain what a thought is, where it originates, how it blossoms into practicality and how it is funneled into a storage area we call the Akashic record.

We have already tried to explain that everything - absolutely everything - is vibration of one sort or another as everything comes from and returns to this prime creative force we call God. We explained that God is star light and light is vibration so God vibrates and as God created everything, he created it from vibration.

To add to the confusion, we break off for a moment to bring your attention to a phrase we frequently use when referring to God – star light.

We use this enigmatic phrase because it is true and we wish to say to you that we will try to explain what star light is later in this book but we use the phrase "star light" to get you used to the idea that God is not some old man sitting in heaven and pouring hell fire and damnation on you but is prime vibration which is prime light - star light.

Star light that you see in the night sky is the light, the vibration, we call God and when you look at a star, you are looking upon the manifestation of God.

As we said, we will explain more fully later.

So, we were attempting to explain thoughts.

God, when he first constructed all that exists, put early man in the 7th and 8th planes or carrier waves that he had previously constructed and these early versions of man were presented with a number of problems that God hoped man would resolve.

Over eons of time, man did resolve these problems because man observed these problems presented by God and, eventually realised that, to obtain answers, he would have to "think" how he was going to act.

We can see a similar effect today in some animals who, either in nature or in laboratories, are presented with problems and have to find a method of resolving the difficulty.

In the case of animals, the problem usually presents itself with how to obtain food and various species - some of them - invent ingenious ways of obtaining that food.

Now, it must be said that in many cases it is a case of serendipity (happy accident) where the animal sees the problem and suddenly, something happens that gives him a clue as to how to obtain the required tidbit.

In other cases, especially in the case of higher minded animals, the answer occurred either "out of the blue" or by experimentation.

We have stated before that nothing can appear out of the blue so we assume that the creature was prodded to resolve the problem by the Archangels that control and guide life.

Now, in the case of early man a similar process was used and, gradually, man developed the power to think.

Breaking off again, you may have noticed that people today are discouraged from deep thinking.

People's days are filled with the infantile emotions put on TV that are there to keep people in a state of permanent childhood.

People are encouraged to be in permanent contact with a few friends using telephones. The object being that, once any exchange of real information is exhausted, the endless exchange of banalities continues, often at the level of a small child. Even the use of grammar is largely ignored thus rendering these unfortunate incapable people from expressing any deep thoughts that would require the use of punctuation essential to make their message intelligible to others.

Thus, we hope that you can see that being surrounded by banalities all day, every day, has been designed by the evil ones to keep you in a permanent state of ignorance and childhood.

We encourage you to reject all this and return to adulthood and the ability to think.

So, the ability to think was placed, alongside imagination, in the 6th dimension which is a very high dimension, higher than, perhaps, you can imagine because imagination and thought are only one step away from your personal aspect of universal spirit (universal consciousness) that is also closely connected to God himself – the source of all wisdom. This explains why the evil ones have gone to such lengths to try to stop you thinking because thinking requires the use of imagination to change those thoughts, which comes as a block of information into a stream of information that the mind can understand.

We wish to expand on this concept of receiving thoughts as a "block" of information for a moment so that you may understand what thoughts actually are.

Thoughts are created in and by the higher self. The higher self, as we have said, is connected to God.

There is only one God and he (it), think of it as you wish, exists in a sphere outside of anything either physical or astral. Nevertheless, God exists.

God is a unique oneness, so all that he created is part of and totally this oneness.

This implies also that there is only one higher self for all of us.

We go back to the concept that we described earlier in which we stated that the 6th plane contained just one imagination for all of us and that any contact with that plane was vibration encoded with our personal vibration to keep it exclusive to us personally.

We hope that you have been able either to understand this or at least accept this as a working hypothesis because we must expand on the concept of oneness and say that there is only one higher self and it is closely connected to the source of all that is that we call God.

That is why we said that higher self was our personal aspect of God, though we failed, usually, to mention that there is only one higher self because we did not wish to confuse you into trying to understand how you could be an individual but the basis of your creation, your higher self, there was only one of.

The uniqueness of all life as one is an advanced concept that not all can grasp at first.

This concept has far reaching aspects, far beyond the number of people incarnate on Earth at the time that you read this.

It implies that all the people who have lived in the past, those who are alive now and who will be alive and in incarnation in the future share the same one higher self and the other aspects that we mentioned previously.

Further, for those who can accept that what are referred to as the heavenly spheres and all the people who inhabit these spheres use the same higher self that you do.

Thus, it is that all life everywhere and any dimension use this one unique higher self and also this one 6th plane, share and use the one unique force we call 'imagination' and share and use the same thought process.

It is only because all of our thoughts are encoded, encapsulated, by our unique frequency that keeps our thoughts unique to us.

Now, we realize that this concept of oneness of being, of sharing the same unique planes of Godness, thoughts and imagination is a very difficult one for many to accept but it is so.

The ability for some to accept that, since the dawn of human existence, to forever in the future and for all and every sentient being in any dimension, we all share just one higher self and just one plane of imagination and thought, is a difficult one indeed.

We mentioned earlier that, in this chapter, we might lose some of you on route and this is one of the concepts that not all can accept.

We speak only the truth as we understand it to be. If you can accept it is a different matter, but we hope you can or will eventually, because the things that we have discussed in this chapter are among the most important subjects we have ever discussed.

An understanding of this chapter of this book is essential to understanding future chapters and about life itself.

Now, we have a problem with deciding when to end this chapter and turn to discuss other matters because understanding what occurs in the 6th plane or dimension could go on endlessly as all events in all areas of life tend to pass through this extraordinary plane but we must stop somewhere.

We have other matters of importance to discuss with you so, with reluctance, we will call this chapter finished - although it is far from finished - and turn our attention to other matters.

CHAPTER 3

THE HIGHER SELF

In chapter two we mentioned a number of things because, as we tried to explain, life is both interconnected as one complete jigsaw but, rather like a jigsaw, life is made up of disparate elements that, together, form the complete picture that we refer to as 'life'. While we were describing the subject of chapter two, which was imagination, we mentioned something called the higher self and said that it was the personal aspect of God. While this is in essence true, the higher self is much more than just the personal aspect of God because, not only is each element that together form life linked in a sort of chain, but God and the Archangelic beings that work for God do not waste energy and so many aspects of life serve more than one purpose – the process that you may know as multitasking.

In this chapter we will do our best to describe the higher self and its various functions but we will also be obliged to mention other elements because the higher self, being 'multi-tasking' is connected to a number of aspects of the spiritual aspect of life.
First, let us say that our primary aim is to describe the spiritual aspects of man but, as all is both connected and one, to mention "man" is also to describe all things from a grain of sand to a galaxy. All is one and although, when looking at a grain of sand, it may be difficult to understand that we are also observing a galaxy, nevertheless, it is so. If all is one it must all be identical. It is only our way of understanding life that makes things appear separate.

So, let us try to examine the higher self and analyse where it came from, why it exists and its functions because, as we mentioned many things serve more than one purpose and the higher self is no exception.

As it so often the case we have great difficulty in knowing where to start in our description of something because, all things being interconnected, this interconnectedness stretches backwards and forwards.
In a previous book called "The Path of Mankind", we went to some length to describe, as best we could, this mysterious force we called God and described how God developed curiosity, the desire to learn, and so invented 8 carrier waves we call dimensions and put life on the highest two (8 and 7) including early versions of man. We also described how the Archangels charged with overseeing the progress of these early version of man put the idea of being able to think in association with them.

But these Archangels, who themselves, had their connection to the God force firmly associated with them decided, one day, to try to introduce into early man a concept that would, like them, enable man to realize his connection to God because, up till that moment man lived in the 7th and 8th spheres or dimensions and was using the 6th dimension to be able to think and to imagine, but had no idea where he came from and why he existed.

Whether these Archangels realized that, one day, man would himself be able to develop to the point that we refer to them as Archangels history does not tell us.

We will also say that the Archangels charged with surveying and helping man's progress are totally different beings to a human Archangel. As is often the case, language does not have words to describe infinitely perfect and powerful beings, one step below God, but these beings are totally different in nature.

One is human highly developed and the other is a being created over long ages out of spiritual matter with absolutely no connection to life as we know it. So, we use the same word – Archangels – to describe two totally different forms of creation.

The Archangels were completely aware of their connection to God and had a space in their makeup where this knowledge was stored. It was, and is, the 5th dimension.

We remind you, once again, that God created 8 carrier waves of dimension that were, initially, totally devoid of anything.

They can be imaged, it you will, like 8 radio or television channels, broadcasting frequencies or carrier waves, but each frequency not yet broadcasting any programs.

As we have said, life was created on the highest frequency – the 8th – then it moved also down to the 7th dimension so that now there was life on both the 8th and the 7th dimension.

Then, eventually, the Archangels chose to put imagination and its various ramifications on the next lowest empty plane or dimension – the 6th – which left the other dimensions still not being used.

As what is referred to as the higher self, which is the personal connection to God, is of great importance, no doubt the Archangels would have liked to have put it on a higher dimension but, as the others were all being used, they placed it in the 5th dimension.

The method of doing this was the same method that was used to create imagination in the 6th plane.

They created a pocket, a file in the 5th dimension, isolated within themselves the frequency of their higher self and created within that file the frequency of high self. Thus the 5th dimension contained the higher self concept as a vibration.

So now, these early men had a bit more to them than just life. They had life, certainly, that they explored in the 8th and 7th dimensions. Also, they had imagination, which they slowly developed and now they gradually became aware that they had a personal connection to God.

No doubt this caused much confusion and head scratching in these early men because it was not easy for them to assimilate into their reality that there was something call God – prime creator – and, indeed, the vast majority of people incarnate today have difficulty realising that they have a personal aspect of God within them and that, in effect, because of this God connection, man is in a way God.

The Archons, who invented religions, went to great lengths to educate people into thinking that humans are just a form of useless creation and that God is an unobtainable force, "out there", always distinct and remote from man. Man's only connection to God being when this tyrannical god decides to condemn man to hellfire and eternal damnation for some fault either real or imaginary.

To say that one is God is considered to be blasphemy.

The Archons have done a good job in pulling the wool over people's eyes and making God a remote and unattainable force always willing to condemn and to whom one must constantly beg favours, just to be able to survive.

However, times are changing and some people are beginning to realize their connection to God and, although God is still a remote perfection, they understand that the higher self provides a permanent connection to this God force and, although we must strive to reach this state of perfection, at least we can say that we are family with God – a father/son relationship – and not master/slave relationship as was the case before.

This relationship is very difficult for some people incarnate and, indeed, discarnate to appreciate and who actually prefer to consider God as a remote being, master of all, and to whom they must grovel on their knees before in a church in the vain hopes that this master will have pity on his poor slaves and spare them the worst that incarnation can inflict on them.

This is not, of course, at all how God operates.

What these misguided souls do not appreciate is that God, although the ultimate spiritual force, actually – thanks to the untiring efforts of the Archangels charged with overseeing creation – works according to physics laws and is not at all impressed by grovelling slaves begging for mercy.

The most fundamental law of physics created by the Archangels is a simple one that we call "The Law of Mutual Attraction".

This simple law, which until recently, was largely unknown to physics experts, simply means that like attracts like and unlike things repel each other.

It has been considered that there are 2 worlds; one of physics masters struggling to comprehend the nature of the world, aided by and abetted by mathematicians also doing the same from their point of view, and the second, the mass of people who, throughout time have struggled to comprehend the nature of life by living it.

It has never crossed the minds of these physics and mathematics experts locked away in their laboratories and lecture halls, to question whether there could and should be any connection between the laws of physics, and far as they understand them, and "real" life.

Even religion, which, supposedly, is there to help common people has created colleges to study the intricacies of the theological dogma and has no idea of the struggles of ordinary people. That is not their concern. They lock themselves away in theological establishments and teach their students of the intricacies of theology, finally unleashing these young priests to administer to the needs of a population that they have never been taught to understand.

This is where the law of mutual attraction comes in, or rather the inverse of it "The Law of Mutual Rejection".

On one side we have physicians and mathematicians and also theologians and on the other, ordinary people battling to survive.

It would have been hoped that spiritual advancement would have helped them to make the connection that any theory that does not include all humanity, indeed all life, must be flawed because, by the law of mutual attraction, we are all one.
It seems amazing that man has existed in one form or another for millions of years and has created miraculous things throughout time, but has never discovered this simple law, the law of mutual attraction, which implies that all life is one.

Before we continue to examine why this is and what it has to do with the higher self we must congratulate the few modern physics and mathematics experts that have started to explore the world of quantum mechanics because, although there was never any need to follow this complicated path, it will, eventually, lead them to discover dimensions and will, in time, lead them to the conclusion that all is one.
Then, perhaps can science and ordinary people be on the same page, so to speak, and life can move on together instead of in the little boxes that life is portrayed as at the moment. Religion, however, is a different matter and we have difficulty in imagining that religious leaders will release the stranglehold that they have over their flock until the flock will see through the illusion and will abandon the churches, which is already happening. Quite where religion will turn to when that happens is difficult to predict. It is not our place to criticize any organisation except to say that any religion that preaches the exclusivity of one point of view, excluding other points of view is flawed and doomed to failure.

As we move progressively into the light filled era, commonly known as ascension, the law of mutual attraction will become increasingly evident and any religion that fails to embrace total togetherness of all and of our father/son relation to God is doomed to fail. This is unfortunate because, as we have said, although religions were an Archon invention designed to separate people and also terrify the members of any church, the concept of following the spiritual path to God is a good one and, if religions can expel the Archon controlled factions that run most religions now and replace them with truly holy leaders, there would be a bright future for religions.
But drastic changes in the infrastructure of most of them would have to occur in order to save them from disappearing.

So, we repeat that all is one from the tiniest grain of sand to the most expanded galaxy, all is exactly the same. Let us then quickly examine and explain what any life force looks like first from a spiritual point of view and then from a physical viewpoint.

At the heart of everything, which is made of vibrations remember, are what we call atoms.
Once again, scientists have struggled for long ages to comprehend atoms.
They have discovered that we can put names to various combinations of atoms and call them oxygen, hydrogen, helium and so on.
There is a table called the "Periodic Table" that has discovered these various combinations, as far as they have been discovered, and have left blank spaces where

scientists predict that more combinations will be discovered and their structure duly noted.

They have also invented very powerful electron microscopes that enable scientists to peer into the structure of an atom.

But so far, they have failed to observe the tiny point of light that shines within each atom.

This is because this light is the light of God that we have mentioned.

Now, this light – starlight – is living. It is life itself.

It is the logos that is contained within each atom.

This logos is actually contained within a protective shell which is called a soul, but this soul is spiritual in nature so does not preclude the starlight of God from shining through.

However, this light can expand or contract according to the emotion that is being projected at it and that evokes a response from the light.

When scientists peer into the electron microscope to examine an atom, it reacts to the emotion put out by the scientists.

It is sad to say that scientist peering at the image project very little joy and happiness.

For a number of reasons their emotions are cold.

So, the light contracts, diminishes, in response to the coldness of the scientists examining the atom.

If those same scientists projected love at the atom and projected love to the electron microscope, the atom would respond and start to glow with light. However, it would take a courageous person to suggest to scientists preparing to examine an atom to sit down and meditate on love for a few minutes. Somehow, meditation and love would make strange bedfellows with science.

The next aspect we wish to discuss is that of how the spiritual aspect of higher self actually works.

Mankind, as we have previously stated was the first and most important of all the creatures that were created.

We also mentioned that all life is one and so, no matter what form life takes; animal, vegetable, mineral, and on what dimension that life lives, it is all, at its foundation, just one life form.

Further, there is just one aspect to any life, by which we mean that if we were to take any object and examine it minutely in all its details we would find that it is all the same as any other object.

We do understand that to look at a grain of sand and to look at a galaxy it takes a stretch of the imagination to appreciate that a grain of sand and a galaxy are the same object.

Further, it takes a stretch of the imagination to appreciate that the human race is just one person and that person is also a grain of sand or a galaxy.

How many of us can realize that we are not only humans but also grains of sand or a galaxy or, indeed, any object or being in any dimension of the universe?

The concept is that God created just one object and that object was actually himself.

The vast majority of people would consider us crazy if we were to propound such a ridiculous story.

However, it happens to be the truth.

But clearly, in our everyday lives we can see that we humans live on planet Earth, surrounded by earth, stones, rocks, mountains, seas, plants, animals, and in the sky, other planets, stars and an endless universe.

That, clearly, is reality because we can see it all and quantify it all, so there can be no doubt that the statement that we are all the same one object is lunacy.

Now, how do we resolve this conundrum that we have mentioned time and again that we are all one unique object called God and all the "real" world that we see around us is an illusion?

This is where spirituality comes in – the 5th dimension.

As we progress in spirituality, as we are multidimensional beings, we develop the ability to tap into the 5th dimension. So we develop the ability to contact this higher self.

When that happens we can start to send out thoughts into that 5th dimension. Do not forget that each and every one of our thoughts are encoded with our unique frequency so each thought remains separate from the thoughts of anyone else who might also be sending thoughts into the 5th dimension.

The higher self is a creation that is a representation of God which means that all the wisdom that God has the higher self also has.

This is very useful if we can question the higher self because this entity – if we can refer to it in such a fashion - has the ability to reply to us.

It does so by sending answers in a block form, a download into our 6th dimension, that of imagination that, in turn, can convert it into a stream of words which can be passed to another part of us which we will discuss later.

Now we said that because the higher self is not only the place where wisdom is stored but is also the place where we get our sense of individuality from.

We mentioned earlier that all is just one thing but the higher self is able to take the logos of God – which is the stamp that tells something that is alive and has approval of and from God to be alive.

Everything that exists that we can see in any area of life is alive, unless, of course, it is a created object such as a robot or artificial intelligence, so it is given this logos, this stamp of approval, that tells whatever it is that it is both alive and also is going to become a certain "something" no matter what it might be.

This "something" could become a grain of sand and "something" else a galaxy.

It makes no difference as all is one.

The higher self creates this sense of individuality in all things but it does not do this randomly. The higher self works in conjunction with a group of Archangels we call the "Directors of Life" who, in turn, work in close conjunction with the group of Archangels that we have been mentioning frequently throughout this book.

The directors of life survey the way life is progressing and the direction in which they hope it will progress and decide if reinforcements are required in any area.

In other words, if more of any particular aspect of life is required in any area.

The directors of life inform the higher self who immediately starts to put a particular logos on any life form so that it becomes that which the directors of life require.

Thus the higher self puts a logos on that something and, if it is a sentient being that can think, the higher self puts this code on the being so that it knows that it is an independent being and also encodes all the thoughts so that they act in the exclusive manner we have described earlier.

Thus it is that the higher self plays a vital role in the development of all sentient beings, particularly man.

The higher self not only creates the beings and things that are required to keep life in balance in a practical sense, but creates this exclusive sense of identify and exclusive sense of sending thoughts and emotions.

But, also, being gifted with all the wisdom that God has, it can receive, question and send answers to anyone who has developed the ability to enter the 5th dimension.

Thus it is possible for a suitably trained person to enter the 5th dimension and link with the higher self and to receive wisdom and answers to questions that might be of concern to the person in question.

The higher self is, of course, capable of dealing with any number of queries, from any number of people in any dimension, simultaneously.

We will also say that, for those interested in channeling or telepathy, either with a person incarnate or discarnate, the communication also passes by the higher self.

Indeed, the process passes by and through the higher self before being transmitted to imagination which, in turn, passes it to the next level.

The higher self, in this case is acting as a sort of spiritual "switchboard", connecting any two people, or more, who wish to communicate telepathically. It senses the unique third frequency that we mentioned earlier and connects the two so that information can pass from one mind anywhere in the universe, indeed the multiverse, to someone else.

Normal thoughts for ordinary people act in a different fashion because thoughts are sent out to the higher self but the higher self listens to the thoughts and either sends them back into imagination unmodified if they are usual, banal, everyday thoughts, or the higher self can take an interesting thought and add some of its own wisdom to that thought before returning to the imagination of the person. The imagination decodes the block of information into an intelligible stream of thoughts which are picked up by the next level until, finally, the person concerned hears the answer to his question as a "bright idea".

So, we hope that you can see that the higher self is much more than just a switchboard, it also contains all the necessary information concerning the person. We call that information the "life plan".

The higher self contains, in what we might consider to be an enormous data bank, the life plan of every person or sentient being, every plant, every planet, every galaxy, stretching back to the beginning and on into the future, plus the life plan of every being on any dimension. This may seem ridiculous but, as we are all one, and if the life plan of any one person is known to the higher self, the life plans and, indeed, the lives of all is known to the higher self.

This databank is what is referred to as the Akashic record.

The Akashic record is contained, associated, within the higher self, which is in the 5th dimension.

So, each and every thought passes into the higher self where it is examined in a micro flash of time, before being dealt with one way or another and then stored in the Akashic record.

It may seem impossibly miraculous that all thoughts from all time and by all sentient beings have thus been dealt with since the concept of the higher self was introduced long years ago, but it is so.

The real world behaves very differently from the world that you live in and there are ways of manipulating the laws of the universe that you could not conceive of at the moment.

This is not to criticize man at his stage of development, it is to point out that science has an infinitely long journey ahead of it until it reaches perfection.

So, we have attempted to describe that there is only one plane of imagination in the 6th dimension and only one plane for the higher self in the 5th dimension.

Once again, as we did when describing imagination, we have not fully described all the attributes of the higher self because there are certain aspects to life that man is unaware of and that would prove too difficult to describe and impossible for man at his level of understanding to comprehend.

We know that this may sound insulting to some especially as we have promised to be open and honest with you. But we hope that you can appreciate that it would be a waste of time and energy to describe things incomprehensible to even the most advanced of you.

But we will still be here for long ages into the future and will complete the picture when it is time.

We have given you enough information concerning the higher self, some of it totally new to man's understanding so we will stop at this point and go on to the next subject for discussion.

CHAPTER 4

THE MODERN ERA

So far in this description of Man's journey through time and space, we have described the move from the 8th plane down to the 5th plane. The first 2 planes or dimensions, 8th and 7th, contained man and all life forms in what we referred to as physical form, although the physical was in an astral sense but, nevertheless, contained life in a manner that enabled it to have a form of physicality. It is somewhat difficult for us to describe states in which something has a form of physicality but that physicality, from an Earthly point of view, people would consider invisible. So, we ask you always to imagine that when we refer to aural physicality we are referring to the physicality relevant to that dimension. So the 8th and 7th planes contained – and still contains – life in a physical sense.

Then we mentioned the next two planes or dimensions, the 6th and 5th and we mentioned that, amongst many other things, these two planes contained imagination in the 6th plane and higher self in the 5th.

Both these concepts have nothing in a physical sense (even astral physicality) to see, so if you could visit one using your astral eyes, there would be nothing to see. They would appear empty but, of course, there is an enormous amount of astral energy flowing through them as every living thing is constantly using these planes to pass imagination and contact with the higher self through. So, we have the top four planes or dimensions fully active.

Now there was a long pause in the growth of humanity before the next phase in man's development came into being.

At this point, we repeat, everything was happening in astral form. The physical world had not yet been invented.

Then a somewhat strange event occurred.

The Archangels, charged by God to help the life forms that they had created in astral forms, wondered what they could do to help God develop even more wisdom.

God, as we said, is the entity that created life but God also developed the desire to experience what his "life" that he had created could do and so he charged the Archangels with the task of creating living forms in the high planes and to present them with problems that they could solve and feed the answers back to God.

We apologise for endlessly repeating this information but we desire for all of you to have as clear an understanding as possible of these complicated procedures and so we feel obliged to repeat ourselves to make sure that you can understand each element in the chain of development.

So, eventually, after a great deal of time had passed, it was decided to create physical life as you now know it.

So, this was the moment of the so called "Big Bang", the moment of physical creation. The moment when this creation came to reality is a long time ago, so you can imagine the eons of time we are dealing with from the first moment that God decided to create 8 carrier waves in the nothingness of astral "space" until the present time. In fact, of course, it would be quite impossible to imagine such a length of time.

We break off from our description of how all the astral forms were created in order to say that we do think that we know how the physical world that you live – 3D – was created but now is not the moment to try to describe the events to you as the story is both long and complicated and so we just ask you to accept, if you will, that this so called reality came into being. We will discuss the events fully another time.

So, the physical worlds, all that you now see on Earth and in the "heavens" (the sky), came into being.
It was not the moment to put human life in this world so a decision was taken first to put animal life (which already existed on the 7th and 8th planes in astral form) here.
But, for that to happen, a planet needed to be fully prepared to enable those animals to survive.
Planet Earth was chosen and "terraformed" with sufficient grass, plants, water and so on that would be convivial to the majority of animals to give them a fair chance of surviving.

We have already described this process in previous talks and published works so we will not presume upon your patience by describing it all again except to remind you that it was hoped by the Archangels that these animals would develop to the point to be able to repay the energy expended in creating physicality, which they failed to do.

Then we also said that the decision was taken to ask for volunteers to incarnate in physicality to help the physical world to repay the spiritual energy that was used to create it all.
By physical world we are referring to the totality of it all.

This is where the story starts to become increasingly difficult to describe. So we will have to take things very slowly and attempt to describe what physicality actually is and just where mankind was at the moment when physicality was constructed – the moment of the so called Big Bang.

We have already mentioned that man was in astral form in the 7th and 8th dimensions and that he had links to the 5th and 6th dimensions or planes as we sometimes call them.
But, once the decision was taken to create a physical universe and once the decision was taken to place life in association with physicality, a number of complicated matters had to be considered and decisions taken.

We have stated that everything is vibration of one sort or another and, so called physicality is no exception.
But, up until that moment, that of physicality being created, vibrations were at an astral level – very fast frequencies.
Any vibration that constitutes something becoming visible must, per se, be of a much lower frequency.

But we have also stated that all life is one. This must imply that all life, up to the highest frequency must be exactly the same as any life of a lesser frequency.

This is the point that we are going to state something that has almost never before been really mentioned nor explained because it flies in the face of any form of logic and we are concerned that, not only will people not believe us but the information that we are about to give will seem to be the words of crazy people.

It was proved by the Archangels who wanted to create physical life to be an impossible complicated act.

These Archangels struggled for a great length of time to work out how to decrease vibration from the very high astral level to the very low level that constitutes physicality.

Finally, the attempt proved too difficult and presented too many problems of how physical life – man particularly – could be at the same time in physical form and also retain his contact with the 5th and 6th planes of astral vibration.

Then, there would be the task of lowering man from the 7th and 8th dimension – extremely high vibrational rates, down to lowly 3rd dimension frequencies.

There was also the problem that all life was contained within the 8 carrier waves which were and are, themselves, astral in nature and of even higher frequency than any form of life that they contained and yet were expected to reduce down in frequency to a point that physical life was contained within the one we refer to as 3D.

So, the concept of creating physical life and a physical universe was abandoned.

This is the point that we somewhat dreaded having to try to explain because it is obvious to all that the universe is very real and that all life on planet Earth is real.

Indeed, we have many times referred to grains of sand, earth, planets, animals, and people and have implied that these were solid, physical objects standing on a solid, physical planet Earth which is in a solid, physical galaxy, itself part of a solid, physical universe.

And now we are implying that none of this is true and that the 3rd dimension is empty because the Archangels failed in their task of putting life here, life which we can all see and touch.

In an attempt to redeem ourselves in your eyes we will say that we have often implied that physical life is a sort of illusion but we have never really attempted to explain exactly what is going on.

In the past, we were always attempting to explain other aspects of life so we touched on that fact that nothing was real – a concept that many of you have been able to accept because it is something that has been known about for long ages, particularly in Buddhism and other Eastern texts – but we have never before attempted to bring you fully up to date with the truth of the matter.

We have, in the past, always stayed firmly in what was already known about life (or thought to be known), but now is the moment to take the giant leap and fully reveal the truth as it will gradually be accepted from this moment forward. That is why we called this chapter "The Modern Era", because it is time to stop living in the past and to move knowledge on to the next step by revealing a lot more about the truth of man, where he lives and how he thinks.

So, once again, we feel obliged to give a brief resume of things we have already mentioned in this and other publications and mention some things that we hope will give you a clearer understanding of what we need to say.

First, we mentioned that God created just one life force but, just to consider man, provided that life force with a large number of individual consciousness so that one has the impression that there are a large number of individual people.

This number of people is the entire number that will ever be created.

But, we must repeat that all these people are actually individual aspects of one object – God.

A way of understanding this would be to consider the vast number of atoms that together constitute an object.

Countless atoms that together constitute one object.

Then we mentioned that God put man on the 8th, then the 7th dimension and linked these people to imagination in the 6th and higher self in the 5th dimension.

You will notice that, from considering the 5th dimension we jumped to the 3rd and mentioned that it proved impossible to place life, including man, in the 3rd dimension.

So, in effect we left man in the 7th dimension.

And that is where all life actually is. All life, including man, still remains in the 7th dimension.

This is information, as far a we are aware, that has never been revealed before.

We believe that those who have described the descent of man into incarnation have skated over where we started off and just went on to portray the areas that we go to in our descent into carnation.

But it is time to reveal to you that; before descending into incarnation we were all in the 7th dimension.

Thus it is that, although man and, indeed, animals have greatly changed over the many years that the history of man has existed, nevertheless man awaits, in the 7th plane or dimension, his destiny to be called forward to whatever journey he decides to undertake.

Now, once again we have to attempt to clarify that there is only one life for all things but, as this life has been given awareness, each and every aspect of this oneness sees itself as independent from every other life form.

So, as we are considering just mankind and ignoring everything else for the sake of literary economy, the 7th plane contains a large number of people all waiting to be called into action.

We must now mention another plane, dimension or carrier wave that we refer to as the upper or higher 4th.

We have often mentioned this dimension and have stated that it corresponds to the heavenly dimension – the place that all return to at the end of their Earthly incarnation and this is so. But the upper 4th is also a place that has other uses. It is, amongst many other things, the place where the oversouls are to be found.

Oversouls do not exist in any "physical" form. There are no buildings where they exist nor are there any beings in charge. Oversouls exist as a concept rather like belonging to a virtual organization of like minded people.

But oversouls play a vital role in grouping like minded people together.

The job of an oversoul is to attract like minded people and nurture them to give them not only a sense of belonging but of helping and guiding them through eternity on the long journey to perfection. Oversouls help create order.

It is difficult to find examples in Earthly life to describe an oversoul but we will try to give a few examples that might help.

For instance, if you take a pack of playing cards all jumbled up they are in a chaotic state, but once sorted into their respective suits; clubs, hearts, diamonds, and spades, they have some order.

Equally, in some schools, pupils are place in "houses" which helps create some order in the school instead of just a jumble of students.

Equally, in military circles, soldiers are grouped into platoons, and companies in order to be able to organize those soldiers instead of just having a mass of soldiers wandering about.

This concept of creating order from chaos is the object of the oversouls.

Now, when it is decided that people are required to fulfill a function, which might be to incarnate, to become what are referred to as aliens or any other desire of the directors of life, the Archangels charged with filling all these roles, a call goes out into the 7th dimension and volunteers are sought for this particular duty.

The people in the 7th dimension already have developed a certain attraction towards a particular role.

In the case of those who might wish to incarnate on Earth, if the directors of life note that they will soon require reinforcements on Earth, the call goes into the 7th plane and volunteers step forward.

The required number are moved down to the 4th dimension and are grouped together in an oversoul. We repeat that the oversoul only exists as a concept so each volunteer is informed that he belongs to this particular oversoul.

These oversouls are usually designed to group together people of a similar spiritual age and with the same interests. It would cause confusion if, for instance, among a group of new arrivals were some of immense age and wisdom. Or amongst a group interested in incarnation on Earth were some who wished to explore the extremities of the universe. So, we generally find – due to the law of mutual attraction – people of similar spiritual age and with similar interests.

Those newly arrived people in their 4th dimension soul groups, after a period of acclimatization, are visited by angelic beings charged with educating these new arrivals to take their place in the world according to their chosen destinies.

To keep things simple let us concentrate exclusively on a group that wish to incarnate on Earth.

Over a long period of time, various angels, each one an expert on a particular aspect of human life would educate this group about life in incarnation.

Other angels would work together with these individuals to choose what is termed a life plan. Readers of this book should already be familiar with life plans so we will not expand.

Eventually, the final stage of development arrives and that is to be given an aspect of the sign of the zodiac.

Once again, we have previously covered this topic.

Now the young spirit is ready to incarnate.

We wish you to fully comprehend that, until that moment, the entire existence of the young spirit was in the astral planes.

First in the 8th dimension, then the 7th with links to the 6th and the 5th and, finally, the 4th dimension.

You may remember us saying that the Archangels failed to put any life in the 3rd dimension – the physical one.

So, we have a problem. The next step for the young spirit should be to incarnate in the physical dimension but that is impossible.

If we could step back and see the 3rd dimension as it actually is, it is just a carrier wave and an empty void.

It is bereft of any life.

And yet you see it as being full of life of all sorts and varieties.

So, what is going on?

It has been mentioned by us and by other knowledgeable people that we create our own realities.

We have also stated that the 3D world in which you live, and that seems so real, is a sort of hologram.

People, generally – those that can accept this concept – pay lip service to the idea but don't really have any idea of what it actually means.

Now is the moment, perhaps for the first time in modern history, to attempt to explain precisely what all this means.

Let us go back to the young spirit waiting in the astral realms to "incarnate".

He would have been taught a great deal about how physicality works, about people's personalities, the good and the bad that can only exist in physicality and also would have been informed that it has been proved impossible to create a physical universe with physical life in it.

This, of course takes us to the point of what does the young spirit do next?

Now, we must apologise to you for not really having told you, in the past, the truth up until this point but it would have been somewhat of a distraction if, in the middle of an explanation about some facet of physical life, we had casually thrown into the explanation a phrase of the type, "by the way, nothing physical exists and the 3rd dimension in which you appear to live is an empty void".

We think you would agree that it would have caused a slight diversion from the subject under discussion so we have contented ourselves up until now with just informing you that life is a sort of hologram and that we are spiritual beings living a physical incarnation and can create our own realities, and have left it to that.

However, now that we have a complete book at our disposal, we can take the time to explain the mysterious world in which you appear to live and hope you will be able to understand and to accept what we will tell you. All that we mentioned previously was to sow the seeds to help you understand the imaginary world around you.

We mentioned that the young spirit stopped at the zodiac signs, which are part of the higher 4th dimension. According to collective wisdom, he would incarnate and associate himself with the body of a newborn baby.
But, as we said, that cannot happen, at least quite in the way that it appears on Earth.

All is vibration and all must stay within the 8 dimensions that God created so long ago. Further, all is one. There is only one life force.
We are as tired of repeating these facts as you must be in hearing us say them, but it is essential to understanding reality never to forget.

So, we must now go back in "time" to the point where the Archangels had to admit failure to create a physical dimension out of astral matter.
As you can no doubt imagine, this must have caused great consternation among the Archangels charged with complying to the desires of God because God had suggested to these Archangels that it would be beneficial to him if there was another level to life – the physical one – from which he could draw benefit and increase his wisdom.

The Archangels are not God's slaves but they are keen to try to help God as much as possible so, no doubt, there was much cogitation going on as they devised a plan to make a "false" physical reality.

They, the Archangels, finally realized that the answer had been there all along. It was the 6th dimension, that of imagination.
If only they could create within all the different life plans, the concept, the false idea, that they were living in a physical reality, make it so convincing that no one would see though the illusion, all life placed within this illusion would behave as if it were a real, physical universe.
As you can imagine this was easier said than done.

The Archangels had to create, from nothing, a sort of theatrical place, a huge stage, in which the players and the spectators, once they entered this theatre, this virtual cinema, would not question it and would accept the scenery and the roles the various characters played as completely genuine.
The scenery was already in place in the 7th dimension and, to a certain extent, the 8th dimension so it was fairly easy to form copies of that scenery, reduce it in frequency and place it within the 6th dimension – that of imagination.

The Archangels tinkered with the scenery until it was as convincing as possible.
It is there to this day. Those "incarnate" call it the "galaxy", the universe that is all around them as they look in the daytime on Earth and into the night sky to look at the planets and stars.
But it all came, originally from the 2 higher spheres which, themselves, had been created eons before to help early life develop.

This imaginary universe that was placed in the 6th dimension, created by reducing the vibrational frequency of that already existing in the higher spheres was done so by the Archangels making a copy of it in their "minds", reducing its frequency and just reproducing it in the 6th dimension.
One way to imagine this is for an artist to look closely at a picture and then painting an exact copy of it. In fact, the artist would be using his imagination to store the image in his mind and then just allowing his mind to release that stored up image.
The Archangels used a very similar method.
They closely observed what had already been created in the 7th and 8th dimensions and then released that stored up memory into the 6th dimension.
This was the moment of the "Big Bang". It was the moment that the Archangels released the image of what they had observed into the 6th dimension.

If what we have explained appears a little confusing, might we try to explain in another fashion, a fashion that many of you who are used to manipulating computers will readily understand.
Imagine that you have a computer and, within one program, you have some information. This might be words, numbers or a picture.
Imagine that you wished to put it in a second program that used a different frequency.
You would copy the piece of information, place it in a program designed to alter the frequency from the original program to the destination program. When this has been done, you would copy once again the altered information and paste it into the second program.
So, the original piece of information remains intact in one form or vibration but now you have a perfect copy of it in a different vibration.
This is more or less exactly what the Archangels did.
They made a perfect – or nearly perfect – copy of the universe created in the 7th and 8th dimensions, altered the frequency of this universe so that it was compatible with that of the 6th dimension and "pasted" a copy within the 6th dimension.

So, we have just explained where the universe you think you live in came from and how it came into being.
Although we have explained this in as clear and simple a fashion as we can, we do realize that many of you will be unable to accept this information and we are sure that it will be many years before the scientific community will be able to "discover" this simple truth.
Scientists prefer to cover black boards with mathematical symbols instead of just reading this book in which we intend to demonstrate to any open minded person that all life exists in and on the 6th dimension and that is the dimension of imagination.
Thus, everything that you think is real is actually just a product of your imagination.

But, we are not finished with our explanation yet. We have other aspects to discuss.

May we repeat just one more time that all this was, and is, happening in astral form. There never was and never will be anything that we could describe as physical in the make up of life.

We feel obliged to restate this because everything that one experiences on Earth seems so real that it is difficult to imagine that it is not.

We got to the point where the Archangels charged with trying to create a physical universe created an imaginary, virtual one in the 6th dimension.

Eventually, they did put animals on it in a vain attempt to let them develop and try to repay the considerable amount of psychic energy used to recreate this virtual world, because even psychic manifestation requires energy.

Anyone who has done psychic work will know just how tiring, how draining this can be so we might have some idea of the vast amount of energy it took to create a virtual universe.

The animals were "imported" from the 7th dimension. As we have previously mentioned, this attempt failed and so volunteers were sought from the people in the 4th dimension to fill the energy gap and the world, much as you would recognise it today, was formed.

We are going to have considerable difficulty in convincing you that the world that you experience from the moment of your birth into incarnation until the moment of your release from it is, in fact, all illusion because it seems so real.

But we must present the truth as we see it and as we know it to be and leave it up to you either to accept or reject this information.

Long before the Archangels tried to create a true physical world, they created a complete script for how life would unfold on this physical world call Earth and how the galaxy and, indeed, the universe would be created from beginning to end.

Nothing was left to chance.

It gives us some idea of the extraordinary intelligence of the Archangels that they were able to visualize, plan and fault find every aspect of every entity that it was proposed to put in physicality, but it was so.

Just look around you now and try to imagine the power of beings that deliberately could have created everything.

Many people think that it was God who made everything but, in the interest of truth we must say that it was actually the Archangels who put together all of it.

As we have said a number of times the original plan failed so we actually do not know what the universe might have looked like had the Archangels succeeded in creating physicality. We only have the illusionary one that we can observe but we must assume that life would have followed a similar pattern in the world that we have to what was originally planned.

Now, the question is, if those humans who had agreed to participate in a sort of play act realized that it was all just imagination would it have been very difficult for them to have taken life seriously?

Any of you who have done any acting know that there is a vast difference between acting – being on stage or appearing in a film – and real life. No matter with what conviction an actor plays a role, no matter how much he tries to identify with the part, he is aware that it is not real and as soon as the scene finishes he returns to his "real" life.

This, obviously was not what God or the Archangels wanted as they needed mankind and even animals to be convinced that the "incarnation" they were going though was as physical as was first designed so that God could benefit from the experience of life having a physical experience.

So, once the training of humanity was complete, the people due to incarnate agreed to have their memory, that life was going to proceed in an artificial manner, removed. This, obviously, has the effect that people born into this artificial 3D think that it is real and act accordingly.

If they could remember that they actually live in an artificial world that they actually create with their imagination, their reactions would be less convincing and so God would gain less from it.

It is the fact that, for enormous periods of time, people think that they live in a real, solid world that has managed to create all the results, all the drama and trauma that has been so educational for God.

But, as we have mentioned before, times change and as life swings into this positive phase, so it has been decreed that the time has come for man to know the truth about where he lives and the world that he personally creates.

So, we wish to make it perfectly clear to you, despite what we and others have stated in the past and may, indeed, state in the future, about life being in two parts: physical and spiritual, the truth is that physicality doesn't exist.

It is all an illusion.

Every aspect of life, man included, is 100% spiritual in nature and the physical world that you think you live in is an illusion created by your imagination. All this is in no way connected to the 3rd dimension which remains for the moment empty.

All life that appears physical is actually connected to the 6th dimension.

So, the best we can say for the moment concerning man's connections to his auras is that he is based in the 6th dimension, has a strong connection to his higher self based in the 5th dimension and has a connection to his oversoul in the higher 4th dimension.

We need to be careful about our understanding of auras and dimensions because it is considered by many that a connection to a higher or lower dimension implies greater or lesser degrees of spirituality and, to a certain extent, this is true but dimensions serve many purposes and there is an area within each dimension that serves to denote our spiritual awareness but we are referring to the parts of these dimensions that serve to provide us with aspects of creation of our bodily parts.

We will deal with the spiritual aspects of these dimensions later.

Let us examine how it is that, once you think that you are born into physicality, you go through your life living in an imaginary reality but that the majority of people pass their entire "incarnation" in this illusionary world that they actually create with their imaginations and never, for a moment, realize that, as it is all just imagination, they could alter the events and actually create a life that would suit them better instead of the drab, dismal life they experience.

There are a number of factors that all work together to keep the illusion in place, some of them created by the Archangels and some of them by dark forces.

It must be said that, if people understood that this so called physical reality was artificially created by their own imaginations and that we have total control over what we imagine, it would somewhat defeat the object of creating it in the first place.

Thus, when you enter this illusionary world, with your mind "wiped", to use a modern term, your imagination kicks in and starts to create the only part that was left intact, and that is your life plan.

Even that is tucked away in the higher self so, until you have developed to the point where you can make contact with your higher self, you cannot make contact with your imagination – in the sense we are talking about – so you just use your mind and your brain to try to analyse life.

But, your mind is not designed to analyse matters. It is just there to implement orders from higher aspects of you.

Let us try to explain how this occurs.

We will quickly mention the chain of existence so you will better understand what we are attempting to explain.

It would be expedient to mention that what we are about to explain is only part of the aspect of life, as life is more complicated than what we are going to say.

But let us state that the chain of events unrolls like this:

1. The higher self which contains the life plan.
2. Imagination: The life plan is passed to imagination and imagination creates the "play" in which you live.
3. The mind that tries to process and put into action the thoughts passed to it from 1 and 2
4. The "physical" brain, which is an illusionary organ that animates the illusionary body.

Now, if all these were fully functional, "you", which is another part – the observer of the play that we call the ID – would have the illusion revealed to you.

So, for the vast majority of people the higher mind is unknown and thus can only operate behind the scenes, pushing the ID down the path of the life plan.

Then imagination, we will say to simplify matters, is split into two parts, rather like the hard disc in a computer. There is the part available to you in order to create things in your life and there is the part unavailable that is constantly operating the "program", the illusionary world that you think you live in.

In many ways, life works in the way that modern computers also work, but we stress that life is not Artificial Intelligence.

Life is analogue – real vibrations – not numeric code.

So, we have the higher self that passes a certain amount of information to the hidden part of imagination and the basic world you see appears before your senses.

But, normally, you are unaware of any of this. It all happens behind the scenes.

Then we have the mind. Now, the mind is just an object designed, initially, to work under the control of the higher aspects and create whatever artificial reality those higher aspects tell it to create. But, as these aspects do not connect with mind, it finds itself in the position of having to try to think for itself, to guide the person. However, it is not designed to do that and so the mind blunders about giving orders to the brain to do this and that with no real idea of what is going on and where it is sending you.

The brain, which also is just designed to follow the orders of the mind pushes the person here and there and neither the mind nor the brain have any ability to direct the person – the ID – in any meaningful manner.

This has created, in the past, now and, to a certain extent in the future, the chaos that we see.

We should feel sorry for our leaders who tell you to follow them as they know where they are going, because they also are as lost as the average person. It is a case of the blind leading the blind.

We break off here to say that the concept that the world in which people live and which seems so real being created from imagination is, indeed, not an easy one to assimilate and even those who can accept it as a working hypothesis can have no concept of the full implications of that idea being fully understood … yet …!

It will become understood eventually and will transform all life as you know it.

It is a major part of the ascension process and, although full realization of its potential is in the distant future, we have introduced the concept so that understanding will gradually grow in the minds of people.

This will be the turning point that will transform the people of the world from asleep to awake, if we may use that rather insulting sounding phrase.

We are aware of the contempt in which the evil ones, who are fully aware of this 6th plane illusionary world, hold the masses.

To a certain extent we understand this although, of course, we do not condone the use of such language.

The mystery schools, which were started in Atlantis long ago, progressed through the Egyptian mystery schools and are still in full swing today, teach what we have said about living in an illusionary world and, more importantly, teach how to manipulate the illusionary world so that they can, in an almost, alchemical, magical fashion, create power, riches and world domination.

But times are changing, as we have frequently said, and the information that was denied to the world for so long is being made public.

However, there is an element to this revealing which causes us some concern.

Certainty, good people, those who are kind and helpful to others, will be given the opportunity to manipulate reality to aid all life but, equally, these concepts can be used by evil or misguided people to create harm so we have to be careful in what we say, what we reveal to the public to cause as little harm as possible.

This is sad because we have so much that we would like to say, so much information that we would like to make public but can't until people change.

Therefore, we are obliged to stop in our talk about the illusionary world in which you all live until it is safe for us, or other like us, to open the door into the methods of manipulating so called matter to create a better world.

CHAPTER 5

INTO SPIRITUALITY

So far in this book we have mentioned a number of aspects concerning the origins of mankind from a similar but slightly different point of view from the previous book – The Path of Mankind – which traced the physical and spiritual aspects but in fairly concrete terms.

We also, in this book took the subject forward almost to completion in what we might term concrete, physical ways but from now on we intend to depart from that and concentrate the rest of this volume on the purely spiritual parts although, depending on one's point of view, even what we might describe as spiritual has an almost physical quality to it because all is vibration and all is one.

Therefore, whatever we describe must always retain a link to what preceded it.

So, to resume.

The Archangels working to please God placed early life on the 8th plane. Then volunteers were asked to go to the 7th plane and, to this day, volunteers descend to this plane where they spend much time waiting the moment when they will be selected to become something. The beings awaiting on the 7th plane are merely aspects of life at that point without definition.

Those that are selected to become human eventually descend to the 4th plane and those willing to incarnate on "Earth" move to the 6th plane for their incarnation.

Once the incarnation is terminated the humans return to the 4th dimension where, generally, they stay as they progress spiritually towards perfection.

We must now seek to unravel the secret world behind all these events that manage to link all beings and all dimensions into one glorious whole for, without all the strings being pulled behind the scenes, so to speak, none of this would be possible and nothing could exist.

The problem, as always, is to know where to begin as all is one and each aspect is an integral part of this vast and intricate machine and all work together ceaselessly that produces a whole – the great work of God.

However, we must start somewhere so let us choose a point of departure.

We stress that we choose this point at random and any other point would, eventually, connect up rather like taking a point on a wheel and going round it until we returned to the departure point.

So, we begin with the moment that God created the 8 carrier waves that we have mentioned before.

At the time of their creation, they were bereft of any life forms.

As we have said, they were separated from each other due to being of separate frequencies.

Now this is, in essence, true but it is not the whole truth. Each band was, in a way, connected to those on each side of it because, as one frequency ended, the next one began. We will use here a phrase that has already been used in a previous work and say that the bands were not separated as in an arpeggio in music but more as a glissando, an octave connected, one note joined to the next in a smooth band.

There was a reason for this which we hope to make clear as we progress through this work.

So, any life form placed on one band – say the 8th – could, if it was so desired, slide down through the other frequencies to the first if necessary.

Or, in the other sense, obviously, from the 1st to the 8th or any part in between.

It is important to understand this point, that all the bands or carrier waves are connected, in order to understand, eventually, how life is constructed.

We also wish you to appreciate that each carrier wave, although constructed of vibrations, frequencies, takes over where the previous one left off and rises or falls, depending on which direction one looks at it, until it matches or merges with the previous or succeeding one.

Thus, in fact, all these 8 frequencies form one continuous octave of vibrations – of light – starting at a very low frequency in the 1st plane up to a very high frequency at the top of the 8th plane.

There are 2 more points we wish to stress.

The first is that within each carrier wave, there are an infinite number of frequencies and also, that each band, although we have numbered them 1 to 8, all have equal power. The numbers we have attributed to them are for the sake of being able to describe them and are, actually, interchangeable. 1 is not lesser than 8, and 8 is not greater than 1.

The various aspects of life were placed in an arbitrary fashion. It is we who have given them numbers to help explain and these numbers do not, actually, correspond to reality. However, having given these carrier waves numbers, we will continue to use them for the sake of clarity.

Next, we wish to explain that all life is connected throughout the totality of the bands. Thus, we can say that all life, no matter what form it takes is connected to all other life because all is connected within the bands by what we might consider to be small tubes.

To clarify, imagine an octopus – an astral octopus – and each one of his 8 tentacles being connected to the bands of frequencies we are discussing. Tentacle 1 connected to band 1. Tentacle 2 connected to band 2, and so on.

Also imagine that the tentacles were actually hollow tubes which permitted energy to be passed from any one carrier wave into the octopus or vice versa, from the octopus into the carrier waves.

Thus, assuming that there is information within any carrier wave of interest to the octopus, it can draw that information to itself and thus grow in wisdom or at least receive the information within any carrier wave.

Obviously, we have used the example of an octopus just to illustrate the point we wished to make. It is doubtful that a real octopus would have any interest in the matters we are discussing and, sad to say, many humans have little interest in esoteric matters any more than an octopus.

But, that is not our concern. We are interested in explaining as simply and as clearly as we can the way life is constructed and leave it up to others to absorb that information or not.
The point being made is that all things, from a grain of sand to a galaxy are connected to the 8 carrier waves so that information can flow in either direction between the carrier waves and the object or person wishing to obtain information.

We have mentioned that these carrier waves, which are also called dimensions, have a vast number of different frequencies within them and we have mentioned that everything is vibration. So, that implies that each carrier wave, or dimension as we will now refer to them, are "multi-tasking" and can perform many tasks simultaneously.
We also mentioned that the dimensions are of equal value, or power, and are joined together in one huge octave of power, of vibration. This implies that every aspect of life, in any manner imaginable is joined. That is part of why we can say that all is one.
So, let us try to join the dots of this puzzle and work out how all these disparate elements work together to create life as we know it to be.

In all these dimensions many things are going on simultaneously and most of it is connected in one way or another to all things. It is important to fully appreciate this aspect of multitasking because many people have the impression that each dimension serves just one purpose, usually of an increasingly high spiritual nature, but this is not so.

Each and every dimension contains many aspects essential to the creation of all aspects of life and much of it is either more or less a repeat of what is contained in a previous dimension or, at least, closely related to it.
This is so that different aspects of life, animal, vegetable or mineral, may reach into them according to the awareness of each species.
For instance, a plant or a stone would not require access to information to the same degree of awareness as a human but, nevertheless, because all is one and all is connected, requires a certain degree of access.

It would be ridiculous and futile if there was only one degree of spiritual information available for all life. It must be obvious that a human, even the most "asleep" of us should have access to information of a more advanced nature than that required by a stone. Yet even a stone is alive and has consciousness and so, in its primitive fashion, has a certain thinking mechanism for which it requires access to the dimensions in order to get answers to its questions.
So, the dimensions contain the same concepts, but in some dimensions these concepts are stated in more advanced fashions than in others.

This idea is repeated in all dimensions and for all aspects of life and would include, not only those living in so called physicality, but through the astral planes as well.

These dimensions, when we consider them to be closely associated with the body of an object, particularly a human, we tend to call auras. But auras or dimensions are the same thing. It is our appreciation of their functions that tends to require the change in name. For instance, if we are talking about an area in a global sense, we tend to call it a dimension but when we are considering it in a more personal sense as being closely associated with our physical body, we tend to refer to it as an aura. But they are the same thing and, if we mention "dimension" or "aura" please understand that we refer to the same thing.

So, our task over the next few pages, indeed over the next chapters, is to consider these dimensions, these auras, and we hope to convey some meaning of them to you.

Once again, where to begin. Perhaps we should start by using the word "aura" as associated with the human body and by saying that all is vibration and all is light so the auras are made of light.

Further we must consider that the auras are alive or, at least, contain awareness and so the degree of brightness of any aura can alter in the degree that it is being concentrated on. By which we mean that if a person selects with his consciousness, often called his mind, a particular aura and concentrates on it to the exclusion of the other auras, that aura will glow more brightly than the other 7 remaining auras.

This has often been illustrated in paintings of holy people with halos around their heads. As these holy people were concentrating on a particular aura, so it shone brightly and was observed by those artists that had a degree of psychic vision and so they depicted this aura as a halo of light.

The reason why it shines more brightly is that it responds to the degree of concentration of the person and so is depicted as coming forward, in a sense, to make the information contained within that aura more readily available to the seeker. It is rather as if the person concerned was shining a torch at it although it is the aura itself that glows in response to the degree of attention it is receiving.

It must be said that the attitude of the person concerned plays a part. A person who is depressed would cause the aura to glow less brightly where as a person full of joy causes the aura to glow brightly. The aura responds to the attitude of the person. That person is not only receiving information from an aura but is projecting his personality into the aura. It is a 2-way communication.

We will also mention that color can be involved. Quite often people who are psychic and can see auras surrounding others notice that a very spiritual person will be surrounded by a bright white light. Those of a loving nature will project pink light. Depressed people cause the aura to shine with a brown light whilst truly evil people will cause the aura not to glow at all and so it will be observed as a blackness surrounding the person.

Perhaps that is the origin of the word "black" associated with an evil magician. We also talk of the "dark arts" and "black magic".

Thus, we find that the aura responds to the degree of concentration being exerted on the aura and also the type of emotion. So, we have degrees of brightness and also color of an aura surrounding a person at all times and the degree of brightness and the color constantly alters as the emotional attitude and the degree of concentration alters.

However, the attentive student will have noticed that the aura that we are considering – 1 of 8 – is personal to the individual under consideration and yet the auras apply to all people and, indeed, all life.

So, just to consider this one aura, how is it possible to link it to a person as an individual and, at the same time, have it available to all, regardless of whether they be animal, vegetable, mineral and regardless of whether they are physical or astral in nature?

The answer lies in the fact that each person has an individual vibration unique throughout time to him.

Further, each thought, each emotion has a unique vibration which not only keeps each thought or emotion separate from any other thought or emotion but those vibrations are linked to the vibrations of the person emitting those thoughts or emotions.

To labor this point somewhat, each and every thought has a unique vibration ascribed to it but those individual vibrations have a marker ascribed to them that connects them with, and to, the individual emitting those thoughts and/or emotions.

Thus, for every person or thinking being at any time and in any dimension, they not only are denoted by having a unique vibration, but each and every thought from any aura or dimension is uniquely linked to that person or thinking object/being for all time from the moments of its conception in the 7th plane until the moment, eons in its future, when it merges with the Godhead and disappears from our sight.

This is an extraordinary number of thoughts, emotions and experiences and they are not only stored in the Akashic Record but are also passed into the Godhead to assist God in his never ending quest for knowledge.

It is, of course, thanks to these unique frequencies that we are able to locate and/or track a person if we require rather as it is possible to track a person today through frequencies emitted by a modern telephone.

It is also suggested that each and every telephone call made or received by a person today is recorded in a bank of supercomputers. One wonders where the appropriate secret service got the idea!

However, in the case of storage of messages in the Akash, none of it is physical in terms of bytes of information and none of it is secret. The information is available to all who have the ability to delve in to the Akashic Records.

It is in this fashion that the life review is conducted. The information is copied from the records in the Akash and is played back to the person destined to watch his life review. Even in the heavenly spheres, all is still recorded. Every alien life force has his whole conduct recorded. Every grain of sand is recorded as is every planet and galaxy.

It seems incredible that everything, everywhere is recorded and has been since the dawns of time yet it is so.

One might enquire how this is done.

As always, the answer is simple once one starts to understand higher physics, that is to say physics outside and beyond what are known as the sort of physics taught in educational institutes, Newtonian physics.

As we said, everything is vibration, frequencies of various sorts uniquely encoded.

Thus, all that is needed is a means of storing these various vibrations or frequencies. These are stored in banks of what we might call transformers. Now, in modern electricity, transformers are generally used to change power in one way to another but in the sorts of transformers to which we elude, the frequencies enter the transformers and are stocked in them.

Perhaps memory banks would be a more understandable term but we use the term transformers because these virtual machines are capable not only of stocking frequencies but also of compressing or elongating them so that a long period of time might be observed in a few moments or, equally, an event might be played back very slowly.

Now, we realise that the term "transformer" might cause confusion but that would be for two reasons.
A modern transformer uses two coils of wire and, according to the number of turns of wire used the voltage is increased or decreased.
Also, the word "transform" means to change; which is why the voltages are transformed.

But, in this sense that we use to refer to transform we are thinking of taking the thoughts or emotions of someone or something – a vibration – and changing them into a spiritual force that can be stored in banks or pockets within the dimensions.
This also will be confusing to many so we will spend a few minutes explaining this.

We have already intimated that dimensions are both multi-tasking and also, each dimension has an infinite number of separate frequencies within them.
Now, we are going to reveal something that, to our knowledge, has never been mentioned in the spiritual history of modern man so, as it will be new to all people, many will have difficulty in accepting this information although it is quite simple.

Within each one of the 8 dimensions, there are pockets, storage areas, for every person.
We have already mentioned that, at the very beginning, God created, with the help of Archangels, a large number of aspects of himself for all types of life.
Thus, just to consider man, a finite but huge number of aspects of God were created.
Thus, from the outset, the number of humans were known.
So, in the dimensions, the same number of storage areas were created so that all the experiences for this number of humans could be stocked.
This was also done for every other sentient life force.

Thus, for everything that we would consider "alive", and which has a unique frequency, a storage area of the same frequency was created in each dimension.
Thus you, we and every person who has ever been brought into active life, plus for all those that are still waiting their turn to be called up on the stage of life, a storage area exists in which to stock every thought, emotion and every aspect of their life throughout all time and in all dimensions.

Each of these storage areas – pockets – are encoded with the unique frequency of every aspect of life and so, each and every thought, emotion, experience is stocked in one of the pockets of one of the dimensions.

This will be very difficult for some people to understand because, although the construct is not complicated, to explain it in simple terms is not easy as it all spreads in several directions simultaneously.

So, we will attempt to clarify one more time just using humans and just one dimension.

So, in the 8th plane a vast but precise number of aspects of God were created – man. The exact number was known.

So, in the 8th dimension a number of storage areas were created corresponding to the number of man aspects of God – the same number.

Each aspect of God was given a precise frequency.

Each pocket or storage area, was given the same frequency.

So, any one aspect of God – man –, could link with is own unique pocket rather like a baby kangaroo can go in and out of a pocket made by its mother.

Further each thought, feeling, emotion or word is given a unique frequency but attached to the frequency of the person under consideration.

Each one of these things are stored in the individual's storage area or pocket throughout all time.

This concept is repeated for all 8 dimensions and for all sentient life.

That is why it is so difficult to explain in meaningful terms.

We feel that this concept was not explained before because man was not ready to absorb such complex knowledge and, no doubt, there will be many today unable or unwilling to accept such bizarre information.

This information, if fully understood and appreciated is of mind blowing significance far beyond the actual physical aspect of an incredible number of pockets, of files, awaiting people's desire to fill with personal information.

These files not only contain the personal information such as the life plan of each individual, but also every thought, every emotion, every action both physical and astral, but also the reactions of every person with whom an individual comes into contact, both in physicality and in the astral planes, before and after an incarnation.

So, in this way, not only does each person have a personal file in which all is stored, but it interacts with the thoughts and memories of each and every person that have been or will be encountered on route through existence.

This obviously works in a 2-way process. A person's file stores all the interactions with every other person encountered and those people's files contain the interaction with the first person.

In that manner the link between large numbers of people going backwards and forwards in time and in space is forged in the most amazing fashion.

The degree of interconnection between huge numbers of people going ever outwards in breadth and ever onward in time has to be experienced to be believed.

One person knows another who knows another and so on in a group sense and the same occurs going backwards and forwards in time, people knowing others who, in turn, know others over generations of time.

Now, there is yet another aspect of this which some may have already picked up and it is this.

As our files are uniquely encoded so, logically it would be impossible to enter someone else's file but, through the fact that information concerning our interaction with others is stored in our file, we have the ability to trawl through the memories of vast numbers of people and over long periods of time. This gives us the ability to draw information about others from our own personal files without straying outside of the limits of our file. Thus, nothing is secret.

The question is, of course, what is the methodology behind being able to link with other people's thoughts?

Like all spiritual things the answer is both simple and complex.

The simple answer is to say that we can link with others in the degree that we have become a complete person.

The complexity comes from understanding what we must do to become a complete person.

In fact, as we are all one, and as we have information about others stored in our personal file, it is a question of being able to reach into that file and retrieve the required information rather like opening a filing cabinet and retrieving the appropriate document. The filing cabinet is our higher self. Now, as we have mentioned before, higher self is our personal connection to God. But it is much more than that.

The higher self contains the information that would be retained within a completely full filing cabinet, each drawer concentrating on any one subject.

So, it would be difficult to imagine a filing cabinet with quite so many drawers but we must use an example taken from everyday life to help you to understand what we are talking about and a filing cabinet was chosen as the most readily understandable object of everyday life. But we wish you to understand that the number of drawers would be virtually without limit and the capacity of each drawer to contain information on any particular subject also without limit.

So subject after subject would be retained within the files and could be examined if we knew how to access the information.

Now, this is where it becomes more difficult to explain and more difficult to comprehend because the process of retrieving information from the higher self involves other aspects of life beyond and above just the higher self.

We need to imagine that the higher self just stocks the information and it stops at that.

But to retrieve a particular file from this vast filing cabinet we called the higher self requires some sort of retrieving system a bit like a well trained secretary or a computer system in which we create a file name and the appropriate file appears.

This retrieval system is contained within the imagination aura – the 6th aura or dimension.

We have explained that the 6th dimension is the illusionary field in which you currently live but we have also explained that each dimension is multitasking. So, not only do you live in this imaginary world but the information contained in the higher self passes through the same dimension before being passed on to your mind and brain for you to be able to visualize.

But, we have suggested that the 6th dimension is the field of illusion, imagination. Thus, it is quite possible that, as the information passes through imagination it can be altered by that imagination. In the higher self all information for all people is the true version of what occurred in any area of life and at any time but, for those able to tap into that information, by the time it has passed through the 6th dimension – that of imagination – that information can, and is, altered to conform with the life plan of each individual person as the ID tries to make the information retrieved from the higher self conform to the unique life plan of each and every person.
So, this is leading us onto the concept that the life plan of each person is but an illusion. We will deal with that concept later as that requires careful analysis.

But we wish, briefly, to recapitulate what we have stated above in an attempt to make quite clear what we attempted to explain.
There is only one higher self for all humans but each human has a unique frequency. So, this vast filing cabinet that we called the higher self contains all the knowledge of all the events throughout all time and of all experiences. But, because of the unique frequencies of all humans, the different drawers in this vast filing cabinet contain only the information relevant to that one person although there are links to all other humans, past, present and future.
But this information contained within the higher self is a true account of events.

But then there is the 6th dimension, that of imagination.
Once again, there is only one 6th dimension for all human life but, through the unique encoding of each person, we all have a unique access to that plane.
But the 6th dimension is that of imagination so, by the time any request for information passes through the 6th dimension and into the ID, it is given a unique "spin" according to the life plan (personality, ego etc., included). Thus, it is that no two people think alike and thus it is that we create our own realities.
It is the "spin", the distortion created by each person's version of how imagination has altered the original information, that creates the unique reality in which each person lives.

So, each person opens his individual drawer in the filing cabinet that we call the higher self, pulls out his file which, in order for it to make sense to him, passes through his imagination and then that altered version is passed to his personal version of the ID (collective consciousness) and the person concerned lives that version of life.
This implies, of course, that even what is called "collective consciousness" is unique to each and every person and no two people would have exactly the same view of the collective consciousness.

All this, we appreciate must be very confusing to many people because much of what we are describing has never been mentioned before and so will be difficult to accept. But it is our desire to describe to you in this series of books the truth, the reality, if we may thus describe it, of how life works and how it is constructed. It is possible that you who read this information might reject it as nonsense but the next generation will realize that it is true and will grow in wisdom through being able to accept what we are saying.

We will just mention at this point that, if you are struggling to make sense of this, imagine the task that Jesus or Buddha, and other saints, would have had to explain these concepts to primitive people long years ago. These saints did their best to explain some of these concepts but it would have been pointless in them spending long hours unravelling the complexities of life to the populations who had absolutely no concept of the points being discussed.
Even today there will be large numbers unable to comprehend.

However, we are not concerned about time and, it must be said, nor are we concerned by who can and who cannot understand, at the time of producing this information. We have been charged with revealing this information and we leave it in the hands – or rather the minds – of others to develop to the point where they can understand.

Even though it is our intention to reveal much new information to the public there remain aspects of life that rest beyond the concept of modern people to understand. This more advanced information will be revealed long years into the future as man grows.
It would be pointless in going into areas far beyond the understanding of people today and we must also say that we do not wish to reveal to the evil one's, concepts that they could turn against us. So, we will go so far and then stop.
Be aware that what we reveal to you in these publications is both true and innovative but is not the whole story by any means.
But, just as we were around at the time of Buddha and of Jesus and helped spread truth, so we will still be here long years into the future spreading cosmic wisdom.

CHAPTER 6

THE ID

Thus, we go on exploring and explaining the spiritual nature of existence.

We have mentioned how life passes through various dimensions and is permanently linked to some of them.

We have, in this book, and in others, tried to explain as clearly as we can how what is called a human, if we ignore his physical form and just concentrate on his spiritual aspect, uses the various dimensions either as staging posts in his progress from and back to God, but how these same dimensions, different aspects of them, are used actually to create what we call man (human).

Indeed, what we called the plane of higher self (the 5th) and the plane of imagination (the 6th) are vital is shaping the personality of man.

But we mentioned that all these planes or dimensions are multi-tasking and can be used for many purposes simultaneously. God wastes nothing.

So, let us turn to another aspect of man that we have mentioned before – the ID.

We have mentioned that the ID is a sort of collective consciousness, that there is only one ID for all of humanity, past, present, and future.

But what are we actually considering when mentioning the ID? And why do we use this strange term?

First and foremost, it must be obvious to us all that we are alive, have the ability to think and have a sense of uniqueness, a sense that we are individual beings.

No matter how much a person attempts to reduce his ego and attempts to join into a collective whole, we always retain our awareness that we are unique individuals separate from any other being or object.

This state of separateness is essential and is a part of our fight/flight mechanism.

But, behind this is something that we could call a greater truth. This is an awareness that we are all one.

Deep within us is the notion that we are all aspects of this one God force and thus are all one with God.

This oneness is what is called the ID.

The two letters I and D were thought of long ago as a means of describing the concept of oneness. It is strange because the modern interpretation of individualism is ID – identity. Everyone has a means of identifying himself as an individual, distinct and separate from anyone else.

In many countries people have "identity papers" or an "identity card" on which are written details of a person's life: date and place of birth, full name, name of parents, a photo, a finger or thumb print and a unique number associated to that person.

Thus, there can be no doubt that we are identifying a unique individual when we look at a person's ID.

In effect, God's greatest creation – man – is reduced to a number, and we call that number a person's identity (ID).

But we have been using the same term for a considerable length of time to describe the complete opposite. The origin of the term dates from an ancient language that precursed Sanskrit and was used to describe not only the oneness of all mankind but its link to God.

However, the origin of the word is of no importance. It is the meaning that is of consequence. At the risk of labouring the point we wish you to firmly realize that we are referring to not only a person but the grouping of all mankind at the highest spiritual level – the 7th plane – and not only is all mankind linked as one person but that person is God. That is why the ID is of paramount importance and merits a chapter of its own.

So, we will do our best to investigate the ID and describe to you its various aspects as far as we, ourselves, are aware.

As always, when investigating life, for man, as you are aware, is just one aspect of life, it is necessary to start at the beginning and return to the 8th plane, where it all started.

We have explained as completely as we could and in simple terms the way that God's Archangels created within the 8th dimension a virtual universe and clothed it with what was necessary to enable the creatures that were placed there for those creatures to have a sense of identity with that virtual world.

Thus, eventually, man – in primitive form – was placed in and on the 8th dimension.

All mankind are aspects of the one creator, God, and so, in reality, there is only one man – God - just as there is only one blade of grass, one drop of water, and one animal form. These disparate objects are all just the one entity – God – the creator of life and God, being a unique life force, created just one copy of himself and put life into it. So, everything is this one life force. We have stated this over and over again but, do so once more because it is relevant to what we are discussing now and will become self evident the day, long into the future, when you return to God.

But, obviously, as we have also stated, this oneness was not at all what God designed in his quest for knowledge.

So, the Archangels created individuality and the world that you know came into existence.

Obviously, there is much more to life than what you are aware of but life is sufficiently complex for the moment and we will not, in this work, discuss alternative realities which are relatively unknown to man at this time.

We will ask that information concerning alternative reality be added as a postscript at the end of this book.

Then will all that we know about this particular aspect of life be more compete but without overloading this book with information not directly related to the subject under discussion, which is the various aspects of auras as they apply to man.

Thus, we return to discussing the ID, the sense of individuality which is, nevertheless, connected to Cosmic or universal consciousness.

As we have already mentioned we are all one but, being one, we would naturally all have the same thoughts at the same time which would be ridiculous. Imagine, if you can that a grain of sand, a blade of grass, a drop of water, an animal and a human all had the same thoughts! It would mean that all would have to think at the level of the most inanimate object. It would imply, for instance, that the most potentially intelligent human would be stuck to thinking like a grain of sand does. This would not push life forward at all and so the Archangels gave to all life the ability to have individual, (as an object, and collective, as a species) thought.

So, what this implies is that humans, for instance, are aware that they are human with an understanding of what being human implies and also each human has the ability to think as an individual.

We will also say that most animals and even plants are aware of their species and of their individuality.

Obviously, less animate objects like minerals – sand, stone etc., - might well have an understanding that they exist as a collective species, sand, stone etc., but would not necessarily have a sense of individuality.

It takes quite a level of spiritual awareness to comprehend the concept of individuality.

There are some species of animals, ants and bees for example, that might well have the awareness that they exist as individuals as well as a species, but are required to try to forget their sense of individuality and work as a group, suppressing any desire to think as an individual and just following any directive the queen ant or bee issues and following that directive regardless of any personal sensations or emotions they might have.

This concept of suppressing individuality has long been admired by some humans who have attempted to create similar modes of living.

Slavery is one example where the slave must suppress his personal feelings and just work endlessly, following the orders of the master.

Military units are another example where orders must be obeyed without question. To challenge the order of the commanders is not tolerated and any person questioning an order is subjected to brainwashing techniques.

There are also a few alien groups which operate under similar concepts. Fortunately, these alien groups are very few in number and their somewhat negative ideas are kept in check by other groups who closely monitor these zombie like entities to ensure that they cause no harm.

So, what we are trying to impress on you is that the ID, this collective consciousness, is somewhat restrictive in nature and it is only our sense of individuality that enables us to progress as intelligent beings.

We also mention this as a warning because political, religious and many other groups that try to "lead" the general population of any, so called, "civilized" nation are constantly trying to force people to conform to their half-baked rules and regulations and would love to have the population of any country all cease to think as individuals and just follow, blindly, any directive they might issue.

We advise people to resist these attempts to normalize populations and for people to retain their sense of individualism.

Therefore, we may think of ID – this collective consciousness – is, in a way, the opposite of individual awareness.
But ID does play an important role in our makeup. It gives all humanity the realization that they are human.
Then, later, it enables humanity to realize its connection to all other life and, finally, it enables humanity to comprehend that there is only one and that one is God.

This concept, that we are all one and that one is God, may be accepted by a number of people incarnate and who have followed our, and others, teachings but, in a global sense, how many people both incarnate and discarnate could accept this reality?
How many could comprehend that a human, an ant, a grain of sand on a beach and a galaxy are one and the same thing and that, collectively, there is only one object and that object is God? Very few, we would suggest.
The Archons have done their work well.
But, as we have mentioned, times are changing and people will start to wake up soon and realize that all is one. When that happy day comes wars will cease when people realize that, when we kill someone we are killing ourselves. When we eat an animal, we are eating ourselves.

We return to our study of the ID, this collective consciousness that actually can cause some confusion as it battles with individuality. Individuality is closely associated with both ego and with the God desire to be the most successful example of the species of the aspect of creation being considered.
To become the most successful aspect of God's creation is, as we have explained in the example we gave of a plant, the complete opposite, in a way, of collective consciousness as that, surely, implies that we are all one and should be able to take into consideration the hopes, feeling and desires of all.
We also discussed and explained this apparent contradiction.
We refer you to the appropriate chapter if you do not understand as we do not wish to repeat that information.

But our concern is an explanation of the ID. It should be obvious that the ID, of which there is only one for all humanity, might well be the sense of cosmic awareness that all life is one but must also contain the knowledge that there is individuality.

So, we have these two aspects operating at once.
We have the desire to be the most perfect example of God's creation and, at the same time, the desire to be part of the whole.
So, we obviously need to explain just how these two opposing elements can be resolved.
This is where we need to mention an aspect of creation that is virtually unknown to mankind, or certainly is seldom mentioned.
It is the God spirit itself as attached to all life. But, as we are considering just man, let us concentrate how this God spirit actually works.

Now, we know that you have already dismissed our previous statement that it was virtually unknown to mankind as nonsense as we have talked about little else but we are not referring to our link with God as we have already described it.

We are talking about a different concept which, as it will be new to you all, will be rejected by many and we do understand that.

We wish to introduce to you an aspect of God that is virtually unknown.

It is an area that is actually contained in association with each individual dimension or aura but is actually attached as a small extra part to each dimension.

As we said, God created all of the 8 dimensions and left them empty.

Then, later the Archangels came along and filled them with life or emotions etc., as we have described in our previous talks.

But what we did not mention was that, at the outer edge of each dimension, God reserved a small part for himself.

Now, how best to describe it?

We could, for example, use the example of a phonograph record in which one track had been left blank for God to use or we could use the example of a computer hard disk where a small file was created and left blank for God's use.

We wish for you to realize that each and every dimension has, associated with it, an area that the Archangels did not and do not use. It is reserved for God to use as and when he desires.

Now, we have often said that God creates life and then leaves us to live that life in order to gain experience that, ultimately, is passed on to God for him to become ever wiser. This is true but is not the whole truth. God surveys his creation and monitors its progression closely. He never abandons us to our fate, although for many it seems so. He watches attentively all his creation – his children – and, like any good parent, leaves us to grow and to try our strengths, learning from both our successes and our failures, but he is always there to help and guide us when we ask.

This is the, apparent, blank track on the phonograph record that we mentioned, the extra part to every dimension or aura.

This blank track is, in fact, associated both to each individual sentient being, and to all sentient life collectively.

This is the part that can explain why we are able to act as individuals – the ID that we mentioned - and also as one being, collective consciousness.

This is the area that enables, when we can contact it, for us to be able to understand how we can be both at once.

The wonderful thing about God is that we can act as if God does not exist but, when we realize that this extra track exists, enables us to be, up to a point, directly guided by God.

We wish to make it quite clear that those who claim to have a direct link to God and to those who claim to be able to channel God, that they may well just be using an aspect of their imagination. God is outside of all that.

Those who can contact this area, and to be guided directly by God, are not those who would boast about this. The public would never hear of such people.

These people would be immensely wise. Truth is to say that, even in the heavenly realms, very few know about this extra God track and, among those incarnate, there are even fewer but, nevertheless, as all auras are attached to all people both individually and collectively, the extra track is there and is available for all to contact.

For such people who can contact this extra track, God can and does advise such people and God can, also advise groups of people.

Of course, the question is what advice can God give above and beyond what we have already mentioned, that is to say, beyond the explanation about how we can be singular and plural at the same time?

The answer is that God is able to give information that would never be available to ordinary people, even the wisest, about how his creation was created. Much of what we tell you is the result of that which God chose to impart to some wise people who, in turn, passed it to us lesser beings who, in turn advise you.

Thus, it seems unfortunate that so many dismiss this information that was, in fact, imparted directly from God into the minds of some of the wisest beings in creation. But all have free will, so all have freedom to accept or reject information in the degree that they can either understand these great truths or not.

It must be said that there are some who are influenced by the evil ones and who are pushed to dismiss this wisdom as the evil forces try desperately to cling to power.

We might ask what is the difference between the higher self and this God track?

The answer is that higher self is used by all people all the time in various ways but this extra track is only available, at the moment, to the very wisest. In time, of course, more will be able to locate this extra track.

For the moment, it remains accessible only to the very few but, thanks to these few, many may benefit from that knowledge.

Thus, we draw this chapter about the ID to a close.

We have attempted to explain how the ID, of which there is only one for all people, past, present, and future, is in a way connected to collective consciousness but how that seems to be in contradiction to our personal sense of identity but, through access, or at least knowledge, of this extra track used by God, are actually linked.

As with all these subjects we could say more but we have given sufficient to enable students of cosmic consciousness enough to be getting on with for the moment.

In later times, when humanity is more evolved we will add to this knowledge but we do not wish to give you any more than is beyond your comprehension at the moment, so we will move on.

CHAPTER 7

STRANGE NEW WORLDS

Let us now turn to consider the aspect of life in other dimensions, for do not consider that life only exists in the dimensions that you are currently concerned with.

We have to be careful in what we refer to as "other dimensions" because we do not refer to alternate realities of planet Earth that we have examined somewhat in an addendum placed at the end of this book.

By other dimensions we refer to copies of the worlds that we have so far described but of a different type of vibration to that which we have already mentioned.

For those who have read or at least perused the information contained in the addendum concerning alternative realities to the world as you know it, you may have noticed that we mentioned that the alternative realities were created as a back up plan should any one reality – including this one – fail. So, spare realities were created to ensure continuity of God's Master plan – life.

In a similar but different manner, a number of alternative dimensions were also created to ensure that should this dimension fail for any reason there were other dimensions to ensure continuity in a dimensional sense.

Perhaps we should explain first to what we refer when we consider realities and dimensions.

Our problem, as is often the case is that language has only so many words that we must use over and again to describe widely differing effects.

By reality we refer to all that we have attempted to describe in the various books, talks and essays that we have presented to you so far even though we used the word "dimensions", sometimes interspersed with the word "auras" to describe carrier bands of basic frequency in which much of life is contained.

While we are talking about our reality we are aware that we did not mention the first and second dimensions or auras because there is nothing that concerns humanity or even any life as we know it in either of those areas but, for the sake of completing this book, we will describe them later.

For now, we have attempted to concentrate our thoughts on those areas of life that do directly concern us.

But we wish to move away from the reality we have mentioned, strange as some of it may seem to some of you, and examine other dimensions. We wish that we had a different word that we could use because we are in no way referring to dimensions that we have already mentioned. Nor can we use the word reality as we have already used that.

So, we ask you to bear with us and accept that we will be talking – or rather, writing – about areas that are real but remote from the aegis of man's knowledge but that were created as safe guards should any other reality fail. One could, perhaps, consider that the reality, in which is our galaxy as we have described it, is also part of this reserve because do not think for one moment that God created this reality as his A team and all other realities were just reserves. God created all equally and our reality, which we must term "dimension" is just one of many.

We hope, for the last time, to remind you that "dimension" refers to all that exists in our realty.

So, now we move away from this dimension and consider the others.

As we mentioned other dimensions were created as reserves should any one fail for any reason.

So, we hope that what we have said so far is not too confusing because we wish you to comprehend that life as we have so far explained is concentrated exclusively in the one reality and we are moving totally away from that and, in effect, starting again in a different area.

Already we must try to explain by what we mean by area.

We mentioned earlier that before all that you now know came into being, there was nothing, only God.

This "nothingness", as we have said is almost impossible to imagine.

But now we ask you to imagine a separate "nothingness", then another and another virtually endlessly.

We do appreciate that if nothing exists, how can there be multiples of it? We do understand that one might suggest that we might divide nothingness into many small pieces and put galaxies in various parts of this nothingness but that is not what we mean at all.

We are suggesting that the nothingness from which our reality is constructed and these other nothingness to which we now allude are all totally different from each other and yes, we do understand that this sounds as if we are writing science fiction but we ask you to expand your mind, if you will, and if you can, and accept, as a working hypothesis, that multiplicities of nothingness did, and no doubt still do exist, each one separate and remote from each other.

In association with each of these nothingness was, of course, God. God is the wonderful being, entity, force that we can't imagine that is, nevertheless, the creator of all that is. Just how much more God intends to create remains to be seen. Already we can say that he has created quite a lot!

But to return to a separate nothingness to the one that God used to put 8 carrier wave bands into.

In a separate nothingness, God put a different system into place. He already had, in his mind's eye, the concept of creating a multiverse based on 8 carrier waves, this one, and so it was pointless creating the same system again and so a totally different concept was created.

Before we can begin to try to describe any new and different dimension we should, perhaps mention that, like all life, any other dimension is based on frequencies but there are a variety of ways in which frequencies can be described.

For instance, in the world that you are familiar with we normally use numbers to describe similar effects. We might use, for example, various actual numbers: 1, 2, 3, 4 cycles per second to describe very slow frequencies or we might call them Hertz to denote the same thing. We might call higher frequencies: Kilohertz, Megahertz, and so on. We might give them abbreviations: KHz, MHz etc. But we are talking about vibrations.

These vibrations might be sine waves, triangle waves, square waves, and so on but always – or generally – we are describing something oscillating above and below a zero point. There are exceptions, of course, but the concept is always a point travelling in time and rising and falling. This is what creates a frequency.

But when we move to a different dimension it would not, perhaps, surprise us if a different form of wave was generated. Also, we might have a different method of describing or measuring any wave.

This is what was constructed by the Archangels charged with creating the various different dimensions.

Would it surprise you, for example, if colors were used to denote different frequencies? Let us imagine that for the equivalent of the Kilohertz range, for example, 1000 different hues of blue were used, for Megahertz many hues of green were used and so on.

This would, of course, just be a different manner of calculating frequencies but would require a radically different mind-set in order to comprehend such a system. It would also assume that the beings living in a certain dimension had a very keen visual acuity to be able to discern minutely different shades of any color.

Of course, we hope that you can appreciate that what we must mention concerning colors was by way of example. In these alternate dimensions it would be quite impossible to describe or for you to imagine the types of frequencies that are used to create dimensions so far removed from anything that is created in our dimension.

Even we, who, thanks to the wisdom of those who help us with these books, stumble in our attempts to describe what systems are used to create these totally different forms of reality.

The problem is that we wish to make you aware of the fact that there exists other realities using totally foreign, to all of us, forms of frequencies and yet, by the very nature of these strange and different realities, we cannot find words to explain them to you.

Even if language did exist to explain, none of us lesser beings than only the wisest would be capable of comprehending.

So, we can only tell you of what little we know.

Let us therefore begin by explaining what we have gleaned about, at least, some of these different dimensions from the beings that have chosen to traverse the gulf from their worlds to ours and have been able to communicate with us, albeit, in hesitant terms, to try to explain their worlds and, in exchange, gain some knowledge about our world.

We are somewhat used, in these modern times, to observe what are termed UFOs (flying saucers) and people have noticed that these machines are far from being of the same form.

Their external appearances differ widely and, from the flying craft that have been captured by various military organizations and have been examined, it has been noticed that their internal functions differ widely.

We should, perhaps, state that not all UFOs come from alternative realities.

First, we should state that some countries have back engineered captured craft and have adapted the technology to human use and so some UFOs observed are actually made on Earth although the origins of the technology used would be alien.

Then we should say that there are a few civilizations that live underground apart from us humans, and some of these civilizations have developed the ability to traverse space in what we call UFOs.

In fact, there are a number of humans that chose not to incarnate in what we call physicality but who have, nevertheless, developed the ability to visit Earth in what appears to be physical form.

If you have understood what we told you about the illusory nature of so called physicality, we hope that you can understand that, as all life is living in astral realms, it is not so hard for people living in just a slightly different form of reality, that is just slightly different in terms of vibrations, to adapt from one frequency to another so as to be able to appear in our world and is not so difficult.

So, if we discount all these various life forms and their flying constructions (UFOs), those that are left must be coming from somewhere else. Some of these are coming from different constructs, different dimensions.

The question is how can we differentiate between the craft that originate in the worlds surrounding ours and those coming from a totally different reality?

Fortunately, the answer is quite simple.

Those that are man made or constructed by human variants generally look fairly solid, that is to say, metallic in construction.

Those coming from a totally different dimension very often appear ephemeral, that is to say, made of light and do not take a solid appearance to our eyes.

The reason is that it is usually impossible for the beings from different dimensions to fully integrate our dimension and, as everything is made of vibrations – light – they are seen as light of various hues.

It must be said that as these craft lack solidity in our dimension it would be impossible for us to capture one and, even if it were possible, the technology used to construct them would not be understood by us and so could not be back engineered by our scientists. They would use physics unknown to us.

Many of these beings are extremely advanced compared to Earth humans, and even compared to those that you refer to as Aliens. The problem is that coming from areas outside of any form of life that we might know, it is impossible for anyone even remotely connected to humanity, as we might imagine it, to comprehend these beings and their technology.

Now would it be possible for us to visit their worlds?
Most of these alternate dimensions are so different from ours that we could not interact with them nor they with us.
However, there are some areas that are sufficiently close to us that they can visit us even though their visitations are in vague, light fashions.
One must always bear in mind that God is light, vibration and the Archangels are also made of light. So, any life forms, indeed anything anywhere, is made of light and so all these different realities must always also be made of light (vibrations). Thus, when seen, they are seen as various forms of light.
Even the beings themselves, if they can assume a form that can interact with our realms tend to be light that is often observed as orbs although some of the entities may have a vaguely human shape as they endeavour to integrate our dimension.

We might question why it is that they bother to come here at all? The answer is quite simply that God wishes to grow in wisdom from all experience of all his creation so God pushes these beings with curiosity about what dimensions different from their quiescent one is like, and thus they try to develop the technology of entering our domain. That way God can develop by observing our realms but from their point of view.
But, as far as is known, there has never been any real communication between beings from our worlds and beings from different realities in the sense of verbal exchange. They occasionally appear in light form, stay for a while and then disappear back to their realms.

We should, perhaps, mention that when we speak of orbs we are not referring to life forms connected to our domains.
We are considering life forms from a totally different reality.

So, what more can we say concerning these beings from alternative dimensions?
We do not have much more information than that which we have already stated.
We feel obliged to repeat, once again, that we are considering beings from totally different planes of existence that have absolutely no connection to any plane that we have previously discussed. Indeed, there are not many people who are aware that there are these other separate planes of existence.
We might well be aware that we have this, so called, physical universe. We might also be aware that there are what are termed "spiritual" areas that we have mentioned in this and other publications.
Some few people are aware that alternative – backup realities – dimensions to our one exist, but very few, indeed, are aware of this further set of dimensions that have no connection whatsoever to any of the aforementioned places.

CHAPTER 8

THE UNRELATED DIMENSIONS

If we wished to investigate areas not readily conceivable to us we would find it harder to find more suitable candidates than the 1st and 2nd dimensions.

We touched, briefly, on those two areas earlier but just said that we would talk about them later. Now is the moment to look into those two dimensions.

We should, perhaps, for the benefit of those who have stumbled on this short chapter without having read the previous ones, mention that, of the 8 dimensions created by God, only the top – or first – 5 dimensions have been talked about.

We mentioned that the 3rd dimension is empty which leaves the second and first to examine.

This will be a rather fruitless examination as these 2 dimensions have no connection to us whatsoever. Nor do they have any connection to any life forms with which we are familiar.

So, what can we say about them?

Perhaps it would be better to start with what we know that they are not.

We know that they are not part of God's master plan for our development in the sense that the afore mentioned 5 dimensions are.

Nor are they linked in any way to the previously mentioned dimensions.

They stand apart and yet must play an important role in God's over-all plan or he would not have created them.

These 2 dimensions concern a different form of life that takes a totally different route to anything that we could imagine and so it will be difficult for us to describe what life is like in these 2 remaining dimensions. However, like all the 5 dimensions that concern us, these 2 dimensions contain life, living entities contained within what we could describe as worlds. However, these worlds and the beings that are contained within them are alive and have the logos of God associated with them much as we do. But the life forms that are associated with these 2 dimensions that we refer to as 1 and 2 have absolutely no connection with anything that we know.

Nevertheless, we will make an attempt to give an overview of our understanding of what goes on in them.

First, let us say that they would be extremely disturbing to us should we visit them as they contain the worst forms of monsters that we could possibly imagine. Some of the life forms are gigantic and are vicious beyond belief. Even in our worst nightmares or drug induced hallucinations our minds would not be capable of creating such beings. The degree of horror created by these entities is such that we would be severely damaged by even a brief contact with the sight of them.

The worlds in which they live are equally horrifying to us.

With the planets – if we can thus describe the areas created by them, for all is created by their imaginations just as we create ours – there is total chaos.

All is horror. The lower 4th dimension in which the angels of chaos reside, pales in comparison to these 2 dimensions.

There is light, unlike the lower 4th which is in stygian darkness, but even this light would cause fear in us because the light actually projects sentiments of terror. The landscapes are unimaginable to us being "jagged" and chaotic.

There is no point in continuing with trying to describe these 2 dimensions because words do not exist to do justice to how awful these planes are.

We have tried to explain somewhat and will just say that Dante's Inferno painting illustrates what life is like there but the painting would need to be increased in intensity a thousand-fold even to approach life in these 2 dimensions.

We must ask why would such horrific planes have been created: God is total love. Associated with love are all the words that follow on from love: Bliss, kindness, understanding and all the positive thoughts imaginable. So, the Archangels charged with creating in the 5th dimensions previously described created the path that all are free to take that would lead to perfect love. But God is interested in all forms of emotions so the Archangels created in planes 1 and 2 the opposite of love. We have tried to give, in the few lines above, what the opposite of perfect love – perfect hate – is like.

This is so that God can grow in wisdom from taking the experiences of these planes and learning about perfect hate. It is not easy to describe in any meaningful fashion what perfect hate is like but it is to be found in these 2 planes.

So, if we take all the 8 dimensions we have the complete picture of life from it's creation until it either finishes as perfect love, with all the phases in between and also perfect hate with all its ramifications.

It may seem extraordinary that anyone would wish to create anything absolutely negative and yet, if we reflect for a moment, we can't really know what love is if we do not have something against which to compare it. Obviously, the opposite of love is hate.

Therefore, it was deemed necessary to create an area where hate could survive and flourish. These 2 dimensions, 1 and 2 are where life in the most negative sense possible is created.

There comes a moment for many of us who have spent a long time in the heavenly spheres and have been able to imbibe the concepts of love, to choose to visit these baleful zones in order to have a taste of just how disagreeable visiting those 2 areas is. The idea is to strengthen our desire to promote love whenever we can because, once we have spent even a short time in planes 1 and 2 and have experienced unbridled hate, it makes us realize how important it is to promote love. It helps us to realize that, unless we work ceaselessly to promote love, hate could gain a foothold which would be catastrophic for all good people and for the development of life as we wish it to become.

So, when we have learned that these 2 negative dimensions exist, and once we have become strong enough psychologically, we ask to be prepared to visit planes 1 and 2. Then we undergo a long process of preparation. This would include talks and lectures by angelic and very advanced teachers who would describe what these planes are like. We would be shown pictures of the monsters who reside there, what you would know as films and videos of the terrain and, finally, we would be given psychic links to machines that can reproduce feelings of hate. This last part is done very slowly, gently and carefully because we have to learn to leave the areas of love that we have, for so long been imbedded with, and learn what total hate feels like. So, this change must be done very carefully so that we can adjust.

As this process takes place, our emotional state is carefully monitored to ensure that we can adjust without becoming distraught.

It must be said that there are some who cannot adjust and the idea of sending them to dimensions 1 and 2 is abandoned. However, most who desire to visit those areas successfully complete their training and prepare to depart.

Even so, none of these people travel alone. They form small groups and have a number of trained guides or monitors who travel with them constantly observing the emotional state of the members of his group. Should anyone become too upset by the visit, they are immediately returned to the heavenly spheres.

For those strong enough, the visit continues until they have visited the relevant areas and have encountered some of the creatures that reside there.

We wish you to understand that nothing can harm the visiting team in a physical sense as all is happening in an astral sense but harm can come in a psychological sense.

Eventually the visit ends and the team, complete with their guides returns home.

It is quite often necessary to hospitalize some people who have visited areas 1 and 2 for a while to help stabilize them and overcome the trauma of what they have experienced, so drastic and dramatic is the experience.

However, like all experience, if it does not permanently harm us, it strengthens us, and most who undergo this most disagreeable experience gain in wisdom from the experience.

We did mention that the dimension just next to the 1st and 2nd – the 3rd dimension – is left blank. It may well be that this was done in order to provide a buffer zone between these baleful places and the 4th dimension.

The 4th dimension is in 2 parts, the lower and the upper 4th. The upper 4th is referred to as heaven and the lower 4th is the place where the angels of chaos reside.

So, we turn our attention back to the lower 4th next.

CHAPTER 9

THE GOOD AND BAD DIMENSION

First let us discuss why the 4th dimension is divided into 2 parts. The higher and the lower. We have often mentioned that the dimensions are multi-tasking. That is to say, they are capable of holding much, often diverse, information and being home – if we may thus put it – to a multitude of individuals of all sorts.

The 4th dimension is no exception, the main difference compared to most of the other dimensions being that, within the other dimensions, one can usually trace a similar path, a connection of one sort or another that links the disparate elements found within a particular dimension together.
The 4th dimension appears to stand out as an exception. On what is considered to be the upper or higher part we find all that is linked to heaven, which we have tried to explain previously in this and other works, and also it contains, in what is referred to as the lower 4th dimension, a number of less than holy creatures.
But, collectively, we call the dimension the 4th.

It may be questioned as to why, when the 3rd dimension is without life should the Archangels, charged with constructing life within the 8 dimensions created by God not use that empty dimension to put negative beings in, especially as it is close to the 1st and 2nd dimensions which we have previously described as containing life forms of the most negative kind imaginable?
The honest answer is we don't know for sure. Like you, we question everything and we search for answers and we do have theories as to why the upper and lower areas within the 4th dimension are thus grouped but, as we do not know for sure we refrain from speculation.
However, we still stress that the upper and lower levels are of different vibrational frequencies and are kept strictly apart.
We, from our more elevated position could enter the lower 4th if we choose, and some of us do from time to time for research purposes, but no entity from the lower region could enter the heavenly spheres. They would be incapable of raising their frequencies to the required level.

We will attempt to explain a bit about the lower 4th dimension, why it exists and something about the beings that live there.
The reason that the lower 4th exists is because, to keep life in balance it is necessary to have an equilibrium between positive and negative particularly in this so called physical reality.
As we have already explained in other publications, if everything lived in physical form for ever and nothing "died" it would result in chaos.
We assume that you understand the concept to which we refer but if you do not we direct you to one of the many talks and comments we have make explaining this for you to have an understanding.

So, to enable "dead" things to decay and for the atoms to be recycled, a force is required that takes charge of causing the breakdown of material matter. Thus, can the atoms be used to create other objects, other life forms thus keeping the cycle of life rotating between birth and death.

So, this is the place – the lower 4th dimension – where the beings that are termed the "Angels of Chaos" are to be found.

Their role in the cycle of life is essential and life as you know it would not be possible without the assistance of these beings.

We used the term "Angels", and they are angelic beings although they do not resemble the positive angels with which you are probably more familiar. Of course, no true angel that works directly for the God force could be imagined and they do not have a physical body such as religions have portrayed them. True angels, whether positive or negative, are totally invisible to any form of humanity, whether incarnate or discarnate but nevertheless exist and play an essential role in the maintenance of life albeit growth or decline.

So, these beings (the Angels of Chaos) are to be found in the lower 4th dimension.

We hope that you can understand that we cannot describe them in any meaningful manner as they do not have a physical form that could be described. Nor is there any human type life associated with them as there is in the higher 4th dimension – heaven. But they are always at work causing the breakdown to its constituent atoms and everything that its useful life has come to an end in the physical planes of the 6th dimension.

Anyone who has been unfortunate to enter the lower 4th dimension immediately is aware of 2 things.

The first is total darkness and the second is a feeling of absolute terror.

We must try to examine and understand why this should be.

In the opposite sense, if one enters the holy spheres, the opposite obtains. When the recently expired people first enter the basic plane (Summerland) of heaven they are immediately aware of light and love. This, as has been previously explained, is because God is both total love and God is star light. So, although in Summerland the light and love of God is not able to be produced at full strength, nevertheless sufficient of it shines and is produced to create the feelings described by those who enter Summerland.

Now, in the lower 4th, as we would expect, we find the opposite.

The opposite of light is darkness and the opposite of love is hate but hate has little relevance in the lower 4th. But what we can feel are some of the subsets of hate; fear, loneliness, and all the attributes that can be imagined as the opposite of love.

The predominate one is fear pushed to its limit – terror.

This one finds oneself in total darkness and surrounded by a feeling of absolute terror.

We wish to make clear to you that these negative beings associated with the lower 4th dimension are not in any way evil, at least not in any deliberate fashion.

They are, many of them angels and Archangels, charged by the creator beings who work directly under and for God, the Archangels we mentioned before, but their function is the opposite of creation – destruction. It is they that cause dead bodies to decompose, any building or object to decay if not constantly maintained.

To help them in their mission a large number of insects and bacteria have been created to implement the angels of darkness' agenda.

In fact, of course, all beings aid in this recycling process by consuming food, absorbing the energy required by them and eliminating the unwanted components in a form that can be used by other plants to produce the next generation of consumable products. Although human excrement is no longer used as fertilizer, generally, it used to be and still is in some areas of Earth.

But manure, as it is called, of animals is still the finest growing material for many plants. Far better than artificial fertilizers.

It may seem strange that each human and animal is actively working with the angels of destruction every moment of every day in the recycling of various food, not only to keep body and soul together, but to provide growing material for future generations of plants. So, in this case of humans incarnate, they work with the angels of creation, enabling their DNA to be constantly modified, as we have previously explained, but also and equally with the angels of destruction who help the body to decompose consumed food which will intimately be recycled in one way or another.

Thus, you can see that both aspects of creation – growth and decline – are equally vitally necessary to the continuance of life as we know it. A moment's thought, for those who doubt, on the effects of what would happen if you consumed food but it was not broken down into its constituent parts by the bacteria contained within the digestive organism would reveal a person unable to live normally. Such a person would quickly become extremely ill and would, in all probability, die if an operation were not performed and remedial action taken.

We hope you can see that the angels of destruction are actually our friends and they work ceaselessly to keep us healthy.

What we can conclude from the above is that, not only are the angels of destruction necessary to the continuation of life as we know it but are just as important as the positive angels. They are the alpha/omega of life. That is why the 4th dimension was used to place both aspects of life within as both aspects of life contribute to the totality of life as we know it.

However, there is always a danger when dealing with negative forces.

Should someone decide to try to manipulate positive forces, contained in association with the upper 4th dimension, the result would be an increase of beauty, surely a positive aspect of life.

For instance, if we enter a garden lovingly tended by a skilled gardener over many years, we are immediately struck with the order, the beauty of the many flowers growing at all seasons and the deep feeling of peace.

However, hidden out of sight, we would find an area where mountains of dead plants and grass cuttings are piled up, awaiting the moment when the angels of destruction will reduce the piles to what is termed compost, the basic elements of the vegetable matter. Thus, a skilled gardener is aware of the balance he must strike between planting new plants and removing dying ones – growth and decline – which continues without cease all the year round, for nature never ceases in working with the angels of construction and destruction.

Where as to work with the angels of construction would create beauty, there are many people who try to harness the powers of the angels of destruction for their personal benefit.

It might be asked, if the angels and Archangels of both construction and destruction are so intelligent, then why don't they refuse to work with negative people causing evil?

The answer is that, despite their wonderful powers, they do not have the capacity to pick and choose what they do and with whom they work.

They were created by higher Archangels – who work directly for God – to perform particular tasks and this they do to perfection. But within their programming, their job description, if we may thus call it, no mention was made of choice.

The positive Archangels work for construction and the negative one's work for destruction.

This they do to perfection.

Here on Earth there are not many people who are aware of the Archangels of construction for the simple reason that there are basically two sorts of humans incarnate.

The first group are the vast majority of the population who are good, kind, decent people but who have no idea of what we talk about in these books, essays and talks.

Then there are a minority that have been trained since time immemorial to manipulate the good people for their profit.

Now, this second group, as we have explained, are those that were taken into the secret schools of long ago and educated by teachers who were themselves under the control of negative entities.

So, they were taught the very things that we now teach you but, further, they were taught to harness the power of the Archangels of destruction.

Through the brutal educational systems of so called education these students often became psychopaths themselves, like their teachers, and thus accepted as normal violent acts against the rest of the population.

So, when they left those schools and assumed their places as leaders of the world's population they, in a way, contained the sorts of brutal, inhuman acts that they were taught about and suffered while at school but were now in a position to inflict – on others, normal people – rather as they, when in the higher classes – were encouraged to inflict on lower students.

This was why the school system for these specially chosen children was set up.

Education about how to manipulate other, lesser people combined with a vicious punishment system which they had to suffer at the hands of teachers and higher students.

Then, eventually, in the last years of their education being encouraged to inflict suffering on lower students.

Thus, they were turned into psychopaths, using the actions of the angels of destruction in their endeavours to create harm to others.

In the meantime, once in power, they manipulated ordinary people by creating slavery, serfdom, the domestic service system, military groups, religious groups which were often compulsory and so on.

At no time were ordinary people told about nor encouraged to use the angels of construction except if it benefitted the upper classes: growing food, breeding animals, creating beautiful furniture and so on.

The lower people might well have been involved in these positive acts but in no way benefitted from them. They lived in poverty and still do compared to the vast wealth that they generate, wealth which goes into the pockets of the wealthy people.

So, it is that the vast majority of the world's population have no concept that they could enrol the help of positive angels to assist them, but the minority understand very well how to enlist the help of the angels of destruction to assist them to rule at the expense of others.

This will change gradually as we move into ascension and the information that we give you is also to help you understand how you can use positive forces to assist you.

So, let us consider how we may enrol the positive forces to help us.

Let us first say that we have to understand clearly the difference between positive and negative intentions.

For instance, most people's first thought goes towards asking an Archangel's help to produce more money. Now, we have to ask ourselves if enrolling the help of an angelic being to create increased finance is positive or negative?

After all, most people could do with a helping hand with paying the bills, going on holiday, putting more or better food on the table, and having better material things.

So, is asking for help with money a positive or negative act?

A moment's thought should tell us that this is exactly what the negative people who run the world do.

If one "goes to work", an employer will only be willing to pay so much for employing a person so no one will ever become rich by working for another. The system does not operate that way.

Equally, it is not every employer that becomes rich through employing others. Some do but many small business people struggle financially as much as those that they employ.

We must also say that not all people are destined to become businessmen and women. It would be ridiculous if all people ran businesses and there were no people left to be employed.

So, that is not the real answer to creating wealth.

Unfortunately, many negative people have realized that working is not the answer so they turn to scheming.

Public finance, amassed through collected taxes, creates an almost unlimited source of finance so many people find means of getting access to this money.

Royalty and those of "noble" birth do their best to get donations from the governments or by delving directly into the state's coffers to provide the resources they think that they are entitled to.

Other people organize contracts to create public works and expect a percentage of the money used in return for giving the contacts to any particular company.

We have cited just a couple of cases in which taxpayers money ends up in the bank accounts of others. The list is endless.

Now, this obviously is negative. So, we can say that to expect an Archangel to assist in creating wealth would be a negative act. Thus, the positive Archangels would not assist in money projects.

So, let us consider how positive Archangels would help us. To demonstrate, the easiest way is, once again to compare the actions of negative people and, thus, negative angelic beings to what we hope would be the actions of positive people and positive angels.

Negative people often, are very selfish. By that we mean that they think more or less exclusively of themselves, their wants, their needs, their desires, their successes and how they can increase all that they desire and the negative angels assist them along this path.

So, we must assume that positive angels would be the opposite of all that.

The opposite of selfish is generous. So, we would assume that the good angels are interested in creating scenarios in which the person who invokes their help is involved, not in helping himself but in helping others.

This may seem futile but you will see the positive results in a moment.

To invoke the positive angels' help we must be prepared to give without regret.

You may be familiar of the passage in the Bible in which Jesus suggested that if a person wanted your shirt, give him your coat as well. If asked to walk a certain distance with someone, walk twice the distance.

Now, why would Jesus have suggested giving precious – at that time – objects like shirts and coats? Today, most people have a wardrobe full of clothes so a few garments are not of much consequence but, in the time of Jesus, most ordinary people probably one had one shirt and one coat so the person concerned would, if he gave them away, be half naked. So, this gives some idea of what Jesus was suggesting people do.

Let us try to analyse why giving a shirt or a coat be consequential in enlisting the help of positive angels.

As we said to give a precious object like a shirt or a coat was a major gift and very few people would be willing to make such a gift.

But, there are some natural laws that may resolve the mystery.

The first and most important one is the law of mutual attraction. This simple law, as we have often stated is of major importance and has been given various names.

Among these is the Biblical one, "As ye sow so shall ye reap".

Now, although this seems to refer to reaping the same crop that was sown, the importance is in the quantity of grains that are harvested compared to the number of grains that were sown.

In other words, if a grain of corn, wheat, rice or whatever was sown, provided the plants were correctly nourished a much greater number of grains could be harvested.

This is thanks to the angels of construction, the positive ones who reward the labors of the farms by repaying his efforts with an abundant crop.

We should, perhaps realize that the angels of construction take the physical and spiritual efforts of the farmer into consideration when they work to produce the harvest.

If, for example, a farmer sowed the seed and then just abandoned it, the harvest would be very poor but, if the farmer carefully prepared the soil, planted the seeds, then lovingly and painstakingly, hoed, weeded, fed and watered the seeds, a magnificent crop could be anticipated.

We hope that you can see from that example that the angels of construction do not simply reward hard work and loving care by replacing – in the case of a seed plant – the one planted seed by another, but reward the farmer by giving (creating) a large number of seeds for each one sown.

This is the nature of positive angels. The farmer, instead of eating all of the seeds of a plant type, saves enough to sow for next year's crop. Then he works on the plants and in the fullness of time, he reaps the reward of an abundant crop with which he can feed his family, sell some, and still have enough left over to sow next year.

We have somewhat labored the point but we did so to demonstrate that, to harness the assistance of the angels of construction it is necessary, first, to give rather as a farmer gives grain to the soil.

Having given, we need also to do what we can to assist, not specifically the person to whom we gave something, but to assist as many people as we can in whatever way we can and then in the fullness of time, we are given a bounteous reward which will help solve our problems.

So, you can see, we hope, the difference between the angels of destruction and the angels of creation.

The first group can be used to cause harm to as many as possible so that one person, family or group can benefit from the chaos and the second type help as many as possible which, through the law of mutual attraction, draws a reward for having given.

The first is taking, which is negative and the second is giving, which is positive.

Therefore, it is easy to evoke the assistance of the angels of construction.

Like the angels of destruction, the angels of construction are always at work and are never far away.

We have got used to the idea that to invoke the negative forces, it is necessary to draw pentagrams and perform complicated rituals.

In fact, to create negativity it is sufficient to ask. However, we strongly advise not attempting to cause harm in any fashion as the price to be paid in remorse and suffering once one has one's life review and goes to hell, far out ways anything one might have received by harnessing the negative forces.

So, in a similar way, to harness the powers of the positive forces – the angels of creation – we just ask them for their help.
But, the trick is never to try to create anything for oneself – after all that is what negative people do – but only ask for help for others.
Then, to seal the pact, it is necessary actively to work to help others.
Then – and this is the magic – the positive angels get to work helping the people we also are helping and the law of mutual attraction draws towards us the very same help we are giving to others.

This is why the master Jesus suggested giving without limit of our help to others because he knew about this law of mutual attraction and he knew that he would reap what he sowed. The more he helped the more he would receive help.
This law worked for the master Jesus and it will work for you.
So, to make it perfectly clear. If you need angelic help, pray for your enemies. If someone requires help, give it unstintingly.
The angels of construction will pick up your thoughts and will help those you are trying to help and the law of mutual attraction will draw help to you.
That way all benefit and there is no harm caused to anyone.

Let us now turn our attention to another part of the lower 4th dimension which is the area that actually contains beings, in etheric or astral form, that can be seen by us humans when we are dressed in our bodies of light i.e.; when we do what is termed astral projection (AP).
Now, we strongly advise all never to attempt to enter the lower 4th dimension because, as we said, it is total darkness but, more importantly emits an emotion the complete opposite of love: absolute terror. Even if one is prepared for this, it is breathtaking – to use a term with which you are familiar – not in a nice sense but in the sense that it is beyond anything imaginable.

The reason for this is that the angels of destruction are to be found there and as they are the opposite of the angels of construction which is light and love, so the angels of destruction are darkness and terror.

But there are creatures that live there. These creatures are negative and are sometimes referred to as demons.
Now, we must differentiate between the angels of destruction which, although totally negative, one could not really call evil as they are doing God's work, and the demonic creatures that are found in the lower 4th dimension.

These demons are many and varied in their forms and in their intentions. The common denominator is that they exist to cause harm if and when they can.

We should, perhaps, ask what is the purpose of their existence?

If humans did not exist in this so-called 3D world there would be no need for demons.

The positive and negative angels – those of creation and destruction – exist to keep the life on planet Earth in balance and exist in a totally separate kind of existence to mankind.

But, when humanity came to be attracted to this physical plane a change occurred.

Humans have personalities and they have free will. They can also be influenced by good or bad forces.

It might be assumed that any and all people would naturally be drawn to do good for their fellow man and for all life but this is not always the case.

Unfortunately, there are a number of people who are drawn towards evil and we have discussed them at some length in this and other books.

Good people are not much of a concern because we can largely leave them to work alone helping all life.

But the people drawn towards evil are a different case.

We must say at this point that evil can take many forms and assume many guises.

We are familiar with children that pull wings off of butterflies and we are familiar with parents and some school masters and mistresses who get pleasure from terrorising children.

Then, of course, evil progress to almost limitless lengths and can involve huge numbers of people. We think of those unfortunate souls thrown into concentration camps for the "crime" of belonging to a different racial group from others and those cast into prisons and become at the mercy of sadistic guards.

The list of evil people is huge even though, thankfully, compared to the total population, it is relatively small.

Now, what has this brief discussion of evil people got to do with demons?

After all, we have stated that evil people will pay for their sins when their incarnation ends and they return to their home in heaven, judge themselves and are drawn by the law of mutual attraction to an area of hell.

Also, we have mentioned the Archons, a negative psychopathic group that influences similarly negative people to cause harm.

Well, man is never alone. Never left to his own devices.

Everyone is guided, not only through an incarnation but throughout the countless years of time spent in the astral realms.

We must also realize that this guidance can take different forms.

Although the concept of guardian angels as understood by most people is not exactly true, there are always angelic beings who overshadow and influence everyone, incarnate and/or discarnate.

We are all one, ultimately, so we are all connected.

Every person, no matter how advanced he might be has someone – sometimes many – more advanced than him to guide him.

But, free will also comes into play. Not all people are holy. There are both holy and devilish people. But they all have guides, angels of some sort or another, more advanced than they are that helps a person along the path he has chosen.

In the case of good people, we are all familiar with the holy angels that look after them but what is not generally known is that evil people also have the right to be guided, overshadowed and influence by evil angels.

So, in the higher 4th dimension we have holy angels who look after good people and in the lower 4th dimension we have evil angels who look after bad people.

These evil angels we call demons.

Just as there are a number of good angels, some more advanced than others, that look after good people according to the person's level of spiritual advancement in a holy sense, so equally we have a number of demons of different levels of evilness who influence evil people according to that person's level of spiritual unholiness.

So, all people are catered for and all are cared for.

God does not judge people. Neither do the Archangels that control all life.

Having given free will to all, the Archangels, who decided to put good angels to guide good people also created evil angels to look after evil people.

This keeps life in balance which is one of the most important criteria for life.

Thus, the demons that are to be found in the lower 4th dimension are many and varied. At the lowest end, those that influence people who are not really evil but we would consider to be very self centered, are simple djinn. They are considered to be demons but are easily controlled by almost everyone who understands the way that demonology works.

But at the extreme other end of the scale there are demons of frightening power.

It is important to understand that demons do not make contact with ordinary people so there is little to no danger of good people ever being influenced by a demon.

The good angels survey good people and keep them from harm.

However, should even a good person decide to do something evil, but the laws of free will and mutual attraction he might open himself to influence by a demon. This would in all probably be a djinn.

The only people who would attract the attention of a powerful demon would be someone who would for many years have been steeped in true unbridled evil.

Just as a good angel help can be invoked to assist anyone that needs help in any manner, so the demonic forces can be invoked to cause harm to a person.

This harm, of course, would be directed against another person. But this can only be done at a price.

To project harm at someone implies that the person who it is intended to receive the harm is informed that evil is being projected towards him and is willing to accept the harm.

Let us explain this. A black magician, if he decides to put a curse on someone needs to invoke a demon to harm that person. However, there are certain cosmic laws governing such events. One of these laws is that to give something to someone, the recipient must be informed that "he is" being given something.

It may be possible to give a physical present anonymously but even then; the recipient must be aware of the present.

For instance, should someone wish to give a bouquet of flowers to another person, the giver may remain anonymous but the recipient must receive the flowers or it would be pointless.

A bouquet of flowers may, usually, be harmless but if a curse is sent – a curse being invisible – the recipient must be informed that a curse has been sent or it would not work.

This is how voodoo, for instance, works. A black magician sends a curse but the recipient must be informed that he has been cursed or he would not know about it and it just would not be effective.

Now, this is a risk. Once a demon is sent to harm a person, not only must that person be informed about the curse but he must accept it. If the recipient refuses to accept the curse it has to return to the sender. This is another cosmic law. A curse cannot remain just floating in space. It has to be received by someone.

Now, in the case of voodoo, the people who practice it are usually fairly superstitious and think that, once cursed, they are doomed to accept the curse and so they do and the pact is sealed. It is rather like someone sending a letter and another receiving it.

However, what a lot of people do not know is that they can refuse to accept the curse just as they can refuse to accept a letter. Then the curse, like an undelivered letter, returns to sender.

So, if a black magician sent a curse to someone and that curse was refused, the curse would have the same effect on the magician as it was hoped to have on the victim.

The demon, once sent on a mission is obligated to harm someone. If he cannot harm the intended victim he will harm the magician who sent him.

This is the nature of magic. It is not really magic but is a form of physics but using vibrations of a destructive nature.

Although simple people involved with voodoo may not know that they can refuse to accept a curse, many more knowledgeable people involved with magic are aware and so would be constantly on the lookout for "gifts" from a known enemy and would under no circumstances accept such a gift. They would be aware that the gift would be the method of informing him that he was being cursed and, quite often, within the gift would be the curse itself. This is not always the case. Once a person has been made aware that he is to be the target of a curse, a demon of some sort may be sent to harm the person in some fashion.

However, as we have said, if the gift is refused or if, for any reason, the potential recipient is unaware of the curse, the demon releases to the sender the harm he was to curse the victim.

So black magic can be a risky business and many a back magician has come to a sticky end through such practices.

Amongst ordinary people today, black magic is much less common than it was in the past but there are still groups of people throughout the world who regularly practice black magic or who hire the services of a magician to harm a neighbour.

Then, of course, there are a surprising number of high placed, influential and wealthy people who belong to covens and who practice black magic, not only to harm enemies but also in the hopes to improve their positions of power and fortune.

As we gradually move into ascension, many of these people will be rounded up and have their potential to cause harm removed.

So, we wish you to understand that we have a sort of double conflict going on in our 3D world.

One part of it is to do with the Directors of Life who keep birth and death constantly in balance – or try to – and humans who, due to free will and their personal desires are battling to impose – due to demonic angels and positive angels – their wills.

Of course, positivity, by its own very nature, is stronger than negativity so evil will gradually decline.

CHAPTER 10

THE ETHERIC DOUBLE

This chapter will deal with the last remaining aura – if we can thus name it – that concerns life in so called physical form. It is referred to as the etheric double. It is seen as a grey/white mist associated closely with all physical objects. Thus, as all is one, not only do humans have an etheric double but all things; mineral, vegetable or animal have an etheric double.
It may be difficult to comprehend that a grain of sand has an etheric double and, equally, a galaxy has one also, but it is so. All is one, so all is the same. Every atom has an etheric double.

Now, let us try to explain what the etheric double is, why it exists and its function in connection with life.
We have already explained in as great detail as possible the human body that, although an illusion, appears real and made of flesh and blood.
We have also described the auras that surround the body and interpenetrate with it.

Now, in order for the so called physical body to connect with these auras so that a two way exchange can take place between the body and the auras, there must be some connecting mechanism.
These connecting points we call Chakras. They are rather like two way valves that allow information to flow from the body into the auras and vice-versa, from the auras into the body.

This two way system of exchange is a vital necessity.
If it was not for this constant interchange, the body would just be dormant because it is the constant interchange of information that enables the body to have the appearance of life and to be a "living", thinking being.

In fact, as we have often stated, the body is not alive. It is only the spiritual forces entering and leaving the body that give it the appearance of life.
This is, of course, a temporary experience and, eventually, the link between the body and the auras is broken and we progress in other fields.

So, although we have expressed these facts often before, we wish to repeat in this book for the sake of completeness, that the physical body is not actually alive. Indeed, it is not even real. It is an imaginary concept created with the help of angelic beings in order to give certain people the impression that they are living in a physical universe.
It is illusion presented as creation. Fiction presented as fact.
But, from our point of view it seems real and we must live as if it is real.
However, the animating energy comes from the auras associated with this imaginary construct.

Now, we do not wish to confuse you with combining illusion with physicality so we will, for the sake of clarity, assume that the body is real and physical. It is easy to see that the auras, being of a higher vibration, are invisible but do exist.

So, we need to find some mechanism that can, not only link the auras with the physical body, but match the energies because, depending on the level of spirituality of the person, the auras can be of a vastly different energy or power than the physical body.

If the auras integrated directly with the physical body and the auras were all, independently and collectively, of a different power than the physical aspect could assimilate, the result would be confusion to say the least.

Now, we mentioned chakras.

Quite often, chakras, in books and presentations on esoteric matters are given great importance. Now, we do not wish to diminish the importance of chakras because they are a necessary element in the construction of human life and, indeed, all life anywhere, because all things have auras and all things have a physical body so all things must have chakras linking the auras to that body, no matter what form it takes.

However, we must also put chakras into perspective.

The physical body lies inanimate until animated by the auras and these auras must, therefore, have some means of connecting to the body.

This is the role of chakras.

Chakras are, quite simply, the means that enables the auras to connect to the physical body so that the auras may animate that body and give it the appearance of life.

But, as we said, there can be a problem and that problem is an imbalance of power between the body and the auras.

Indeed, there is often an actual imbalance between the various auras themselves and, as we implied, to allow the auras to connect directly to the body would, in many instances, cause chaos and mayhem in the body.

The chakras are, of course, simply the means of connecting the auras to the body.

A simple analogy would be to imagine them as plugs connecting electric wires to an object – a house, for instance.

Now, how can we balance and equipoise the auras both between themselves and collectively to the body?

This is where the etheric double comes in.

The etheric double, seen as a mist surrounding as person, is actually a sort of transformer.

It understands the level of spirituality of a person and matches that power with the power coming into it from the auras.

We hope that the student of esoteric knowledge reading this book will have sufficient knowledge to know how many auras there are and how many chakra points there are.

For those who do not know, we will say that there are seven chakras, each one connected to the end of an aura rather as if the auras were electric wires and each chakra was a plug, connecting the wires to the physical body.

This is the function of the etheric double.
The auras do not connect directly to the physical body. They connect to the etheric double and, as that etheric double acts as a transformer, it either boosts or reduces the power of each aura before passing that auric signal to the body.

We wish you to understand clearly that the etheric double is able to accept all seven auras, boost or reduce their power until all are at the same level and at an overall power that the body can accept which it then separates again and passes to the body at the entry points that are described in esoteric literature: namely the root chakra, the sacral chakra, the solar plexus chakra, heart chakra, throat chakra, forehead centre chakra and the top of the head chakra.

Now, it is important that all this energy entering these chakra points from the auras via the etheric double should be equally balanced. That is the job of the etheric double and it constantly monitors the power flowing from the auras and into the etheric double and is always active doing its utmost to balance these seven separate power sources and matching them, not only between them, but at a power that the human body can accept.

We should perhaps say that the same process is going on in every object, animal, vegetable or mineral, but we do not wish to complicate matters by considering these life forms and so we just consider humans.

However, and unfortunately, our human emotions can play a part in the power being accepted into the body.
In a perfect person, the power entering the body via the etheric double would be in perfect equilibrium but how many of us are perfect?
We could for instance consider that masters such as Jesus or Buddha were perfect, but an investigation of their lives would reveal that they, too, struggled to reach that point of perfect balance.
For us lesser mortals, we tend to go through life with one or more of our auric elements out of balance.
We have all met people with an overdeveloped sex drive, or an overdeveloped sense of ego, drive for power, money and other worldly concepts.
Some people are very kind hearted while others we call heartless.
Many have addictions to alcohol or drugs and so on.
All these are signs of people with the inflow of auric power out of balance.
In certain cases, this imbalance can cause illness, and often does.
Perfect health can only be obtained in the degree that our auric inflow is harmonious.

So, it is important that the student of esoteric knowledge try, through meditation, to balance his auras. It is also important to learn to listen to the body and to recognize when something is out of balance and try to correct that imbalance by not giving into the fault until it dies though lack of nourishment.

If we do not give way to anger, jealousy, addictions, the desire for power over others, the drive for money beyond that which we need to survive, and so on, gradually we can aid the etheric double in bringing balance to the body and mind.

Then, and only then, can we truly become the perfect beings that God made us.

But it must be said that if we were perfect we would not have incarnated in the first place.

Apart from the few wonderful beings that incarnated to teach us, the mere fact that we have, or have had, an incarnation implies that we are not perfect.

We include us of the GWB in this comment. Some of us have more or less achieved perfection but most of us are still struggling to reach that stage.

So, we should not be too hard on ourselves. The fact that we incarnate implies that we have deficiencies and incarnation gives us the opportunity to meet these deficiencies face to face and overcome them, if we so desire.

Some people make this effort and are rewarded by a happy, contented life while others cling to their faults as if they were assets.

We think of politicians, for example, who spend their lives expounding half baked theories that their overdeveloped egos drive them to expound.

We think of very rich people who, nevertheless, chase after yet more money in an endless desire to make sure that they have sufficient to keep the wolf from the door.

So, we think that you can see quite easily, if you look at both your body's desires and your thoughts that are out of alignment with what we would consider to be more in line with perfection, and make some effort to correct them.

However, life is meant to be lived and there is no point in shutting oneself away in a cell somewhere in an effort to avoid temptation. Indeed, that would not resolve the problem at all.

We need to ignore temptation not remove ourselves from it.

If we can ignore temptation, gradually it will fade from lack of nourishment as we have stated above.

This simple process is the key to ridding ourselves of our negative aspects.

So, as we do not like having voids in our make up, in the degree that we can rid ourselves of negative thoughts, so positive thoughts can move in to fill the void. It is in that way that we can become better people.

We do not actively have to struggle to become better.

It is sufficient to remove negative thoughts and our higher self will automatically fill the void with positive elements. It is not difficult.

Thus it is that the road to perfection can be trod in the degree that we rid ourselves of imperfection.

It is a natural path that we take. In the degree that we reduce negativity, positivity floods in.

All great saints knew this and encouraged us not to give in to temptation.

The path to perfection is not hard. It might seem to be a struggle but that is because every moment of our waking day is filled with things designed to create negative thoughts.

Some of these we have already discussed in previous missives: adverts on TV designed to create jealousy, sports designed to create fear, anger, and disappointment if our team loses, the constant fear of lack of money, the constant chase after being a more beautiful or handsome person, the constant desire to have a better partner or, indeed, to find a suitable partner.

This endless stream of events portrayed on TV; the political battles, the wars created throughout the world etc., has been carefully designed to keep people in a state of negativity.

The answer is to reject all this, accept one's life as it is, and let the positive, joyful aspects flood in and enable us to rise to a higher level.

This, in part, is what is called ascension.

The evil ones want to keep us all in a negative state, a state of fear, anger and all the negative emotions. When we can see through all this negativity and see it for what it is, just a plan created by negative entities and fed into the minds of our rulers who, in turn feed it into our minds, and in the space created when we reject this negativity, allow positive thoughts to come in and then a wonderful thing happens. Our body and our auras start to glow in a bright manner. God's light – pure star-light – comes with positive thoughts and raises our vibration.

All of every aspect of us, our body, our mind, our imagination and all the things that we have described above start to glow with God's light.

Our ID – the real us – starts to glow bright. As all is one and your ID is actually also everyone's ID then the ID of everyone starts to glow brighter and everyone is affected by the feelings of positivity.

That way, all rise in frequency. Light is vibration and vibration is frequency and frequency is what makes a dimension.

It is through the simple act of ignoring temptation in all its forms, reducing and eliminating the negative thoughts, that humanity as individuals and as collectiveness will be flooded with light of a higher frequency.

By the law of mutual attraction, we are drawn to a dimension that matches our frequency. If and when we can raise our frequency we are drawn by the law of mutual attraction to a higher level, a dimension higher than the one that we currently are on. This is ascension.

As the evil ones are stuck on a low dimension they ardently want us all to stay with them so they can control us and it is their constant fear that we will see through their ploy and reject negative thoughts because, if and when we can rise to a higher frequency, they lose their grip, their stranglehold over us and we are free from them.

That is why TV, radio, the newspapers are full of stories designed to create negative thoughts.

If and when we can rise above them, we are lost to them and they have no one to control. We are free.

And all this can be created quite simply by refusing to accept negative thoughts. It is that easy.

Ascension is the inevitable result of ridding oneself of negative thoughts.

Freedom, joy, happiness, brotherly love is the reward given by God for ridding oneself of negative thoughts.

Then we progress through the dimensions that lead to freedom. This is the only path.

It is not possible to progress while one's life is filled with sin.

Bad habits are not God like habits, so we all need to rid ourselves of them if we wish to advance towards perfection.

Once we can start to rid ourselves of negative habits, which we all struggle to do, we can actually feel that we become better people and if someone has psychic vision and looks at us they would actually see the light shining from us.

That is the light that painters of saints saw and they depicted it as a halo of light around the head of the saint. In realty, of course, that light would project from the entire body. This is the light of a higher dimension.

Now, we wish to add a rider here. Even if you manage to rid yourself of your faults, please do not expect your life to change in a dramatic way.

You will see a difference but you are still here in incarnation and you still have your life plan so you will still be confronted by the many challenges that incarnation presents.

However, as you will now be operating from a higher level than so called 3D, you will find it easier to deal with problems because, as matter is all illusion, from a higher perspective you will find that, to a certain extent, you can manipulate that matter so that life does not seem to be crushing you as it may be doing today.

It has been said that problems can only be resolved from a higher platform than the problem itself.

This is true. It is spiritual law.

So, for many reasons, it is a good idea to try to rid oneself of one's negative faults.

As we said, this is not easy and we, too, struggle for do not for one moment think that the end of an incarnation resolves the problem.

We arrive in heaven exactly as we were on Earth only minus the physical body.

The struggle to remove faults goes on endlessly. As we rid ourselves of one fault, we see that there is another that was hidden but that we now become aware of. So, the battle to rid ourselves of our faults is actually the integral part of walking the path towards God.

As we deal with each fault, so we advance spiritually and the day we no longer have any faults is the day that the journey ends. But that day is a long way off for all of us!

But there is always a reward given by God to us for each fault that we can cast away.

That reward is a feeling of joy and the light of God floods into us in ever increasing intensity.

God is love, joy, happiness and all the positive emotions and it is only our faults that blocks the light.

So, if and when we can remove a negative aspect of us, a fault, so that allows the light to shine more brightly on us.

This applies as much while we are incarnate as discarnate.

Indeed, because of the nature of physical life it is easier whilst incarnate to face and to cast off faults.

In the heavenly spheres it takes much longer and requires more dedication.

So, we suggest to you who are incarnate that you make some effort to cast off negativity and, not only will your life whilst incarnate become better, but it will enable you to arrive in a higher sphere of heaven when your incarnation is finished.

Thus, we say to you who have read this book so far and have, we hope, studied the information contained in the other books we have given you and the various messages that, despite the study of life in all its various aspects being somewhat complicated and intertwined, as far as you, and we, are concerned our task is simple.

We just need to concentrate our existence on removing our faults.

This simple act has led many people in the past and, no doubt, in the future into the arms of God.

However, we live in an age where, generally, people are much more curious about life in all its aspects than in the past and we must say that an essential aspect of progress towards God requires a mastery of esoteric knowledge.

Thus, we give you this knowledge and leave its assimilation in your hands.

We have given you sufficient information in this volume concerning auras and other related aspects for you to sit and connect the dots, as the saying goes, and we hope that it will expand your knowledge concerning the mysteries of life for we are of the opinion that there should be nothing left as a mystery.

For far too long has the world been kept in the dark concerning life, which has enabled superstition to flourish and also the less than good people create and maintain a stranglehold over the world through religions and secret societies.

We hope that a solid foundation of knowledge based on fact and not on superstitions or imagination will spread throughout the world cutting through the haze that has for so long existed which was encouraged through ignorance of the facts of life.

This book contains a treasure house of information on many aspect of life – some of them new to mankind incarnate – and we hope to continue to reveal yet more knowledge in other books in this series until a complete compendium is formulated that will enable all students of esoteric to use as reference works.

We have revealed much knowledge to you in, we hope, an easily understood fashion despite some of the subjects being quite complex.

We have absolutely no desire to bamboozle you with complicated explanations. Indeed, our aim is always to explain things in a manner that the least educated, the least intelligent person can understand.

We look forward to the time when these books will be faithfully translated into as many languages as possible and made available world wide.

We look to the day when all God's children everywhere have access to the same information that we give you.

So, we ask that you study carefully this book. You link it in your mind to the information that we have already given you and, by using your God given talents try to piece the information together in a fashion that is understandable to you all.

You will find that, although each book is a separate entity, and each message that we have given you exists in its own stand alone right, in fact they all link together as one giant compendium and should be thought of as such.

Not one message, not one page of these books, can be considered as out of context with the totality of the information already presented, and will be presented in future works. Any information that seems out of place will be due to miscomprehension on the part of the student, not an anomaly in the information imparted.

So, we end this volume on auras and its related subjects here.

We appreciate that some of the information may seem new to you, complex in some ways and may take some study to comprehend.

We have covered the subject of auras, dimensions, call them what you will in a fairly comprehensive fashion but we wish to advise you that this is not the end of the subject. All life everywhere is connected, so the subject of auras cannot really be considered in isolation from all other aspects of life and we wish you to understand that there is more to life to explain and so we will continue to release knowledge as and when we can until each and every student of the esoteric has a complete compendium for his reference.

So, we seal you in the name of the Almighty and send you on wings of light.
So let it be.

ADDENDUM 1

PORTALS AND ALTERNATIVE REALITIES

Let us first discuss the subject of portals as far as we can separate them from the subject of alternative realities. It is not easy to do because, by their very nature a portal is a passage between 2 realities – if we may thus describe the imaginary areas that we all live in.

So, first let us say, as we have stated so often before that nothing is real. All is an illusion but the illusions are so convincing that, when we are involved in them, it all seems real and so let us imagine that all dimensions are real. Otherwise the whole discussion would be meaningless.

Therefore, in the 6th dimension there would be countless sub-frequencies all created by adding to the base frequency of the 6th dimension, which is a carrier wave of a particular frequency or vibration, a large number of other frequencies of very similar vibration to the quiescent frequency of the 6th dimension but each sub frequency of a unique and slightly different frequency to that of the actual carrier wave frequency.

So, we wish you to understand that, just to consider the 6th dimension, it has a carrier wave that we might term Alpha.

Within that Alpha carrier wave are created a vast number of other frequencies: Alpha+1, Alpha+2, Alpha+3 and so on in an almost infinite pattern.

Thus, each frequency is unique compared to any other frequency or compared to the base Alpha carrier wave.

It is important to comprehend this because each one of these sub frequencies, Alpha+1, Alpha+2 and so on contain life and contain the subject matter of this discussion.

We will describe that life in a moment.

For now, let us try to describe the method of transferring our consciousness from one wave or frequency to another higher or lower.

These different frequencies themselves have sub frequencies within them. So, at the risk of confusing you we will attempt to describe a sub frequency thus: Alpha+1+a, Alpha+1+b, Alpha+1+c, and so on. Now we are aware that there are only 26 letters in the British alphabet but, evidently, there are many more than 26 sub-sub frequencies. We should say that the alpha numeric description we gave was just by way of explanation and it is not used in reality.

The point that we wish to establish is that the different frequencies contained within the sub wave that we termed Alpha+1, start where the previous one left off and slides up in frequency to a certain point where the next sub frequency takes over and thus these sub frequencies are all joined in a glissando of vibration starting at a low level and rising smoothly ever higher. The actual frequency has no importance in terms of power.

The important point is to realize that there is a carrier wave that we refer to as a dimension and that, within that, there are an almost infinite series of sub frequencies which, in turn, contain an almost infinite number of other frequencies.

But they are all connected in one enormous glissando of connected frequencies.

Thus, if we know how, we can easily move from one frequency to another by just raising our frequency; not in the sense of having to step up or down as if we are on a staircase but more in a sense of being on an escalator sliding up between levels.

So, what has this long and somewhat confusing introduction got to do with portals?

As all the different frequencies are interconnected, we are constantly moving up and down these escalators without realizing it. It is part of life to move into and out of these different frequencies.

Indeed, each one of us actually lives on a separate frequency from everyone else. That is what gives us our sense of being a unique person. But these frequencies upon which we live are so similar that, if we mix with families, friends, or work colleagues we don't notice much difference. It would only, for instance, if a person from a European or American city environment suddenly found himself mixing with, say, an Amazonian Indian group deep in a jungle that he would start to realize the vast difference between his way of living and thinking and the way that the Indian people live and think.

They are living in a different world and we can clearly appreciate that.

But, even in these extreme cases, the vibrations are sufficiently close as to be virtually accepted as aspects of the same one culture.

Having explained all that, we will proceed to explain about vastly different aspects of the 6th dimension.

What we mentioned above, if we may return to our alphanumeric examples, implies that the first group all live on the Alpha+1+a, Alpha+1+b, Alpha+1+c vibration. The a, b, and c refer to each individual person incarnate on planet Earth.

But what if we transformed our consciousness to Alpha+2, for example? This would be a totally different aspect of the Alpha carrier wave.

So, this aspect, Alpha+2, we would consider to be an alternative reality.

This is where we need to consider portals because portals are the connecting mechanism between what we called Alpha 1 and Alpha 2.

Thus, nature has provided this sliding mechanism, this escalator between the two aspects of the 6th dimension.

But a portal never opens automatically. Portals only open at the request of someone on one side or another of any 2 dimensions or sub frequencies. In other words, someone in Alpha 1 would wish to go into Alpha 2 or vice versa before a portal will open. The most obvious example is in the death experience where a portal between the person on Earth and the heavenly sphere opens and the consciousness of the person travels along a "tunnel of light" into the heavenly sphere.

This tunnel of light opens at the request of the "dead" person and allows him to leave his physical body and travel through the tunnel, not walking, but moving as if on a horizontal escalator until he reaches the heavenly dimension, at which point, the person steps into the second dimension, Alpha 2, and the tunnel collapses.

The person who makes this journey may not have made a conscious request for the tunnel of light to appear but, nevertheless, he does so – his higher self sends the request and so the portal appears.

In the case of a NDE, when the person is sent back to his physical body, his higher self sends the request again and the tunnel reappears and he returns to physical life.

The problem that can occur with portals is that, generally, they are opened at the request of a visitor from another dimension that wishes to come to Earth and these portals are kept open for a while until the visitor has finished whatever he came to do in which case if someone enters this portal by accident or design he will be whisked off to the origin of the portal and find himself unable to reappear in our world, so he remains lost in whatever place he finds himself in.

This is the case in some forests where these "staircases" appear. They are actually portals opened by various beings or entities that desire to visit. As forests are secluded places they make ideal places for these visitors to arrive as, generally, they can remain open for a relatively long period of time without being observed by any human. But should anyone come across such a portal – which his mind translates into a structure, although it is a portal, and is foolish enough to climb – he will disappear into another dimension and be lost to mankind. Thus, humans should never attempt to enter a portal. Almost certainly he will meet an untimely fate.

We will go on talking about portals and say that they can be just fairly short connecting points between 2 fairly close areas of alternative time/space or they can stretch for vast distances, many, many light years of distance. As time/space is all illusion and these portals are created consciously by entities that understand the great illusion, they can be traversed in a flash of time. The entities that come from these alternative dimensions are fully aware of the illusory nature of "reality" and so are able to manipulate time/space to help project themselves, not around our galaxy – in which they use a different technique, but to move between dimensions.

It must be clearly understood, if any of this is to make sense, that the so called 3D "reality" is one thing – locked into a set of advanced physics – but dimensions are a totally different aspect of life.

If we may give a very childish analogy, imagine that you lived in a totally flat Earth. You would only be aware of forwards and backwards, left and right.

But if someone suddenly points out a new dimension, above and below, it would appear very strange and difficult to comprehend.

This is the case with dimensions. They are a different aspect of reality only recently thought about by those following quantum physics.

But these different dimensions were part of God's original creation and are a fascinating subject that we will try to explain shortly.

So, we wish to conclude this short discussion on portals and draw the strings together in the hopes of bringing understanding to you.

Portals are communication devices that can be created by desire in order to move from one dimension to another. They are actually created from astral matter.

A strong desire can gather sufficient astral matter together to make a passage between two dimensions possible.

They can be visible or invisible to human eyes.

There is nothing really esoteric in them. They are just astral matter collected and concentrated by the desire to make them exist.

Actually, that is all anything is. Everything that can be observed; animal, vegetable, or mineral is just astral matter concentrated to form whatever a consciousness desires. Portals are no different.

We will go on now to discuss the various dimensions and, more importantly to this discussion, what are known as alternative realities.

The connection between the various aspects of so called reality is always a tenuous one due to the fact that all people create their own version of reality using their aspect of imagination and so no two people are living in the same reality and, therefore, should they reach into a different reality it would be one personally created by them and thus different from any alternative reality created by anyone else.

So, in theory, it is pointless in attempting to generalize in any description of any aspect of life because it would really be necessary, before describing anything, to say "In the opinion of Mr. X or Ms. Y, such and such a concept occurs".

Now, this occurs because, as we have stated above, within any dimension, there are a large number of sub frequencies one for each person.

This also applies in the plane of imagination so each person creates with his imagination the world or reality that he considers appropriate to him or her. However, there is an exception to this rule.

The plane of higher self – the 5th dimension – contains truth. It is the only dimension so to do but, to live in this one true world implies access to the higher self.

We have mentioned that there is only one higher self for all people so, if two or more people are able to link with the higher self, any subject that they might mention would be identical as they both would be accessing the truth.

This truth would be coming from the God sphere and would not be open to interpretation as it is the fundamental truth from which all grows.

But, throughout the long annals of history, of the vast amount of information disseminated by huge numbers of so called wise men, scholars and sages, how many have truly been in contact with their higher self?

This can open the door to collective misinformation generated by entities of less than good intent but have nevertheless persuaded vast numbers of people that it is truth.

A classic case is reincarnation and its bed fellow, Karma.

The vast amount of the world's population accept reincarnation as fact and so, if one gathered a large number of people together and asked them to raise their hands if they believed that reincarnation was fact, even today the majority of hands would go up.

Even though it is not true at all.

Thus, we warn all that just because something is accepted by the majority does not mean that it is truth coming from the higher self. It can also be misinformation planted in the collective subconsciousness.

With this warning in mind let us at last turn to examine alternative realities.

Now, as we said, there is no "one" reality because we all create our own reality based on personal and collective experiences and our reactions to those experiences.

But let us, for the sake of trying to understand alternative realities, imagine that we all live in one reality.

Even this needs qualifying because those incarnate would have one set of experiences whilst those discarnate would have a totally different set of experiences and thus a totally different aspect of "reality".

But, we must make some attempt to draw all this into one common denominator or we shall never be able to advance with this subject.

So, let us put aside our differences and imagine that we are all living in a similar world and having similar experiences.

Now, why should there be other realities and what purpose do they serve?

The world is a complicated place and so we need to stretch our minds if we want to comprehend it.

Even though we all live in our unique reality, these realities are sufficiently close that we can consider them to be part of one reality no matter if we are living in the so called physical planes or the heavenly sphere.

One is a continuation of the other.

But, when the physical world was created, the Archangels charged with creating it in the 6th dimension were concerned that it might not function quite as was hoped. So, as a precaution they also created in the 6th plane a number of variants of the world in which you live. This was actually quite easy as they were already working in an imaginary field and they had at their disposition an almost limitless number of bands of different frequencies in which they could place other imaginary worlds.

So, they let their imagination loose and created a vast number of other versions of the Earthly world with which you are all familiar. Some closely resembled planet Earth and others differed widely.

Then they placed within these worlds beings of various types that they gathered from the 8th and 7th planes.

There were, and are, a vast number of diverse life forms in those planes and they – the Archangels – used their intelligence to match the beings they placed on any planet to the type of planet or galaxy that they had created with their imaginations.

So, if one enters these alternative realities one finds life forms, some similar to those to be found on Earth and some so different that they would be difficult to comprehend.

So, these different and diverse alternative realities are all to be found in the 6th dimension and are, themselves, just as imaginary as the world you all live in, physical or heavenly, although, as you are aware, they seem very real, so for the point of discussion we may assume that they are real.

Most of these worlds operate by similar rules to the one that you find yourself in but not all do.

The Archangels let their imagination spread far and wide in creating these alternative realities and so some of them are so different from anything that you would be familiar with that they would be impossible for you to live in.

Now, we must address specifically for a moment those living in physicality.

It has always been imagined that the physical 3D world known as incarnation is a different form of life from the astral worlds and we have been guilty of suggesting this ourselves.

However, the truth of the matter is that physicality does not exist so, what you think of as physicality is but an illusion.

In fact, all life lives permanently and uniquely in the astral realms. Therefore, should someone be incarnate on Earth, disincarnate in heaven or in one of the alternative realities it is all taking place in the astral realm of the 6th dimension and it is only different frequencies that separate the areas.

The heavenly sphere, which is the 4th dimension is, indeed, a separate plane from the 6th but, nevertheless, the people who are in that dimension retain a link to both the 5th higher self, and the 6th imagination. People in all dimensions are obliged to use both the 5th and the 6th dimensions regardless of what area they "live" in.

Thus, it is relatively simple, when one has learned to raise or lower frequencies, to move from one reality to another.

As was mentioned, if someone in one dimension requires to visit another, he decides which dimension to visit and, once the decision taken, gathers astral matter together and makes, with his mind, a connecting tube or portal between his world and the chosen destination and he projects himself down the tube and he appears at his destination. Once his visit terminated he repeats the exercise in reverse and he returns to his home planet.

Therefore the subject of alternative realities is not quite as mysterious as is usually portrayed.

It has been people's misunderstanding of reality that has caused the confusion. If people believe that 3D is solid matter it becomes extremely difficult to appreciate that it can be manipulated.

Once we realize that it is all vibration, all illusion and all connected it becomes easier to realize that it can be manipulated.

It has been suggested that people living in the 6th dimension, that we called Alpha+1, would have an alternative existence on other dimensions that we might call Alpha+2, Alpha+3 etc.

This is not so. Apart from the fact that all people incarnate have a "physical" body and also a spiritual or non-physical body and also the fact that these bodies are being created and destroyed billions of times a second, it is not true that we have countless alternative realities in other dimensions.

This, once again, is a smoke screen created by evil people to confuse others.

If one goes to another reality, the beings observed there would each be on their unique vibratory plane just as all life is here on Earth but one would not encounter duplicates of oneself.

There would be no point in doing that. Life was and is created on these alternative dimensions as a sort of back up plan, a security in case life here failed to prosper.

But the life forms placed on these other dimensions are unique, each one to its own dimension. Thus, if life died out on any dimension a new set of life forms could continue on the next dimension.

Thus, we can realize that each dimension exists as a unique and separate space in the grand universe that the 6th dimension is, but it is important to realize that these dimensions are, in a way, connected because as one dimension ceases the next one begins. There is no break in the different dimensions. They proceed ever onwards from the first to the last in one long glissando.

This being so, it implies that it would be possible for a person either by accident or design to travel from one dimension to another by just altering his current frequency from the Alpha wave he is currently in into an adjacent Alpha wave.

Then, as he travelled through this new Alpha frequency he would notice an increasing difference from the world he left to the new world he has entered.

It needs to be understood that, if a person slides from his Alpha wave into an adjacent one, it would at first seem very similar to his home wave or planet. It would only be as he traversed this new Alpha wave or planet, that life would start to be dramatically different as he approached the next Alpha wave on the far side of the wave that he was crossing.

One might question how this would apply to our Alpha wave so let us examine just planet Earth to see if there is any difference from one side to the other side (from one frequency upwards or downwards in frequency).

We tend to accept planet Earth as it is and don't question the vast differences that there is just on planet Earth. But we might live in a temperate zone, or we might live in an extremely cold one or a very hot one.

We might live on dry land or in a water environment, in a volcano or in caverns deep under the Earth.

There are many areas, each one separate from the others and each one of a different vibration.

So, as we approached the frequencies where our Alpha galaxy touches a different Alpha frequency above or below it in terms of frequency so whatever the type of environment that exists at the point where the new Alpha touches our Alpha, the environment would attempt to be as close a match to the new Alpha as possible.

We appreciate that a verbal description of this relatively simple explanation may be difficult to understand and a drawing would better explain but we only have words at our disposition so we do the best we can with words.

The point of that somewhat convoluted explanation was to tell you that the joining point between any 2 dimensions or realities would be very similar. It is only as one progresses through the new reality that the landscape alters.

Now, if one could progress through alternate realities, one after another, Alpha 1, Alpha 2, Alpha 3 and so on, so the reality from your base Alpha vibration would become more and more noticeable.

Eventually, of course, one would arrive in a reality so different from one's base Alpha frequency that it would be impossible to progress further.

Some of theses alternative realities are strange indeed but it is worth remembering that they were created, initially, as back up to ensure that what is termed physical life could continue in one shape or form.

This creation was a long time ago and now each reality has created a reality of its own and exists in its own right just as our reality exists as an independent, positive creation.

Now, it has been questioned if time travel is in any way connected with alternative realities.

As you know, time does not exist in reality. There is only the "now" moment. So, in theory, time travel is not possible.

However, it is obvious that in the illusionary world in which we all live, time has always existed and is considered to be an integral part of history. Even in the heavenly spheres we mention the past, present, and future.

So, let us try to examine somewhat what we mean by time and how it came to exist. At the time when, originally, God's Archangels created life in the 8th plane, time had no relevance. Everything being immortal, there was no need to consider time.

But, eventually, life developed to the point that the 6th dimension was filled with a variety of different elements, one of which was and is the illusionary physical universe that you people live in. So, in that area the concept of both space and time were introduced. We must say that both space and time are illusions, as we have often stated in the past but became an essential part of this false reality.

We will also say that sequence of events, which is another way of considering time is also an illusion, although we have often mentioned it as a sort of replacement of time because all things actually exist at the same moment. But we must have, when dealing with the so called physical universe, something to latch on to, to help explain how life appears to work in the world in which you live, so sequence of events was chosen to replace time in order to help you all get used to the fact that time does not exist.

So, if time does not exist and even sequence of events is an illusion, how and why do we need to have time in the illusionary worlds created within the 6th dimension?

The answer is fairly simple although rather difficult to explain and to comprehend. Time has to be connected to another illusion we call space. In recent studies time has been irrevocably linked to space by some mathematicians and physicists and has been called "space/time". Both are illusions but both appear real in the illusionary world that you live in.

When life was placed within the 6th dimension, it was understood that carnivorous animals would need to feed themselves. Thus, the concept of the strong hunting the weak was introduced. There were certain advantages in this as Darwin described in various publications. It was, and is, called survival of the fittest.

Quite simply, it means that if an animal can learn not to be eaten before it can reproduce, the knowledge of how to survive would be included in his genes – his DNA – and be passed to his offspring.

So, the concept of fight/flight was also introduced.

Any animal being attacked by a larger animal intent on eating the former so that it also might survive, has one of 2 choices.

Either it fights its attacker hoping that the attacker will itself abandon the idea of eating it or it runs away, hoping that it can outrun its attacker.

To run away implies having space in which to run.

Thus, we hope that you can see that the concept of space, and eventually, space/time is linked to fight/flight.

This, quite simply, is what the concept of space was created for.

Obviously, over time, when humans were introduced, the concept of space was largely expanded because humans, having a different form of intelligence to animals, once the basic concept of survival was overcome, turned their attention to examining areas outside of their immediate area in which they live.

Animals, generally, remain within a quite small area which they learn to know very well and stop at that.

Apart from the relatively few species that migrate, most animals do not concern themselves with areas outside of their home base and certainly do not stop to consider what the moon is, nor the sun, nor the stars in the night sky.

It is only man who concerns himself with that.

So, we will say something that will shock many.

As we all, animals and humans, create our own realities we can hypothesize that, before humans were introduced, much of what now exists did not exist. As animals were not interested in the night sky, for instance, it did not exist.

Just as many animals are not really concerned by the concept of night and day – either sleeping through the night time or sleeping through the day time - the concepts of either night or day do not really exist in many species. If diurnal animals are considered, for instance, as soon as dusk arrives, they return to their lairs and sleep until daylight appears, when they wake up again.

They have no concept of the night, nor of the moon, nor of the stars.

If woken up, they would be totally lost if they were forced to leave their lairs at night.

The same applies, in reverse to nocturnal creatures.

Thus, as all is created by imagination, when only animals lived on Earth much of what humans accept as normal – stars for instance - did not exist. There was no need for them and so they were not created by their imaginations. Even the moon did not exist.

Nocturnal animals developed eyes that could see in the relatively total darkness and/or developed psychic ability to see the auric forms of their prey.

If we could go back to those early days, the universe that you are accustomed to seeing would have looked very different from what it does today.

As animal life spread around the planet, so large tracts of Earth were developed through imagination.

The interesting aspect of this is that skilled people have come up with the theory that, long ago, planet Earth looked very different to what it does today and, although these experts have no concept as to why planet Earth looked different, the simple answer is that it did so because all life creates their environment with their imagination and, if there were no sentient, thinking beings in an area, that area did not exist.

Eventually, as you know, man volunteered to "incarnate" in the 6th dimension that you know also as your dimension.

Now, we have described, somewhat, in different talks and publications the long years that it took man to develop to the point that one would consider really sentient.

We will not describe why humans who had spent long years in training in the higher 4th dimension for an Earth type incarnation were so primitive at first but we will do so eventually.

But, we fast forward to the point where man was capable of understanding somewhat, not only physical life but also started to get an inkling of his spiritual aspects.

It was at this point that the moon was brought into its present position. We have already discussed why this was so.

The point we wish to make is twofold.
1. That man is in two parts – in theory at least, if not in practice.
2. The vast number of people who still have no real idea of the spiritual aspects of all life.

This second part is the reason that space/time must continue for long ages.

If it were possible for all people, indeed all life, to realize their divinity, there would be no need for killing and thus no need for time/space to exist quite as it does, because time and space are linked to the fight/flight aspect of many life forms, including man and thus we are tied to this vicious circle.

However, as has been mentioned, we are moving into a long period of peace and so, the concept of killing will gradually fade and, difficult as this may be to comprehend, the notion of fight/flight will diminish and ultimately disappear and so the notion of time/space will greatly alter.

All is one and so it will be possible for all things to live as one.

But while we are talking about time/space as it exists now and of perceived reality, we would like to mention a couple of things that science has recently noticed and causes people to ponder.

The first is that quantum mechanics has formulated that, until an atom is observed, it doesn't exist. We hope that we have answered that question in various talks and documents.

The second is that the universe is expanding.

Once again, the answer is simple.

If nothing exists until it is required to exist, by the same token, if we search we will find. Thus, as astronomers explore the outer edges of the galaxy they question, in their minds, if there is more, and thus they create more in their imaginations.

It is necessary to realize that many of these alternative realities live by different rules to the ones applicable on Earth.

Some may have notions of fight/flight and thus space/time associated with them but many live by different rules indeed to those applicable on Earth.

It would be fruitless to try to describe these worlds because, not only do words not exist to explain the notions, but you would be quite incapable of understanding the methodology of such life anymore than the creatures living in these strange worlds could understand life in our world.

But, as we have previously stated, here on Earth there are vast numbers of people that would and do reject our teachings as totally spread by rambling minds.

It is time to wrap up this talk about portals and alternative dimensions.

We have given sufficient information to enable you to understand the nature both of portals and alternative realities.

We hope that this explanation gives you food for thought and has helped to clarify yet another aspect of God's great creation – life.

ADDENDUM 2

THE OTHER SIDE OF LIFE

This will be information concerning life in other dimensions than what we have so far described.

We have mentioned life in two different dimensions or areas of existence but there are an almost infinite number of areas where life exists.

We wish at this time to describe life in an alternative version of Earth to that which we have mentioned.

We have described life in the 6th plane – that of imagination – and we have described life in backup versions of life created in case any one version was destroyed or failed for any reason.

However, there is a version of life that is very close to the physical one that you are familiar with and in which you think you live.

We wish to describe to you life in an area that few people are aware of but is interesting to investigate. It is a version that will become apparent in the future as people progress through ascension.

It is to be found as one progresses outside of and beyond the solar system as it appears in this life.

If and when we can develop our intellect to the point that we can realize that all is illusion and that nothing really exists, not even the one point of light that we and others have mentioned – this singularity – we appear to be left with nothing.

Indeed, we have mentioned that higher self and God is to be found in this apparent nothingness and we have mentioned that there are multiples of this nothingness each one working towards the creation of alternative versions of life as we know it to be in our galaxy.

We might have given the impression that God – prime creator – is to be found in these nowhere places. Whilst that is true, it is not the end of the story.

If we can, with our minds progress beyond the nowhere place in which God is to be found, we can come out on the other side of that nothingness into a whole new creation.

It can be imagined if one counts back from certain number towards zero, 5, 4, 3, 2, 1, 0. Then start to count in negative numbers -1, -2, -3, -4, -5, and so on.

Whilst the life that we are going to describe has nothing to do with numbers, positive or negative, it is worth using numbers as an example in that mathematics can progress beyond zero.

It is worth noting, in passing, that Roman numerals did not have a sign for a zero and certainly did not have negative numbers and so, we imagine that had we been born at the time of the Romans, some 2000 years ago, to suggest negative numbers would have totally confused people.

We, today, are used to negative numbers and there are even those versed in imaginary numbers.

The point being that, today, negative numbers are understood where as 2000 years ago they were not.

So, as we have no concept today of life on the other side of God, so to speak, a start has to be made somewhere and, hopefully, one day, the concept of an alternative life will be accepted.

Let us hope that it does not take 2000 years to become common knowledge.

Yet another way of thinking of God is to imagine a circle with God at the centre.

If we can visualize that life, as we know it with all its ramifications, is taking just half of the circle, it leaves the other half for this alternative version.

After all, if God really is this being of infinite creative power, why should he not be able to create an alternative version of life?

However we visualize it, the fact of the matter is that there exists an alternative version of life following similar rules to our life but in an opposite sense rather as we have one half planet Earth lit by the sun whilst the other half is in darkness.

So, could we describe this alternative version of life?

Could we visit it, and if so, what would we see?

As we have already intimated, we can only start to investigate this alternative, diametrically opposed aspect of life when one has developed a great deal of knowledge both spiritually and scientific. However, thanks to those beings who have reached this stage and who have explained to us what they observed, we are able to describe it to you. We must express our deep and undying gratitude to these advanced people who have shared their knowledge with both us and you because, thanks to these people, we are able to bring to your attention information that has largely been unknown until now.

Knowledge is power and it is through power that we can break the stranglehold of ignorance that has been used to keep humanity in slavery for so long.

Thus, even if you have difficulty in believing some of what we tell you, we suggest that you read carefully all the messages that we give you, some of which are being revealed for the first time. Then, as you advance and as you come across this information you will be able, more easily, to accept it as truth. The first barrier – that of creating a pigeonhole in which to store information – will have been broken.

Freedom comes in the degree that we can accept truth.

So, let us start by repeating that which we have already explained which is that, in the degree that we can reach into the higher self – which is also God – we can, eventually, come to a place where God is to be found.

This place is outside of time and space. It is presented to us as absolutely nothing. A place where nothing at all seems to exist.

Already, this is difficult, indeed, to describe in any meaningful terms. It has to be experienced in order to understand.

Language exists to describe space, time, physical and even mental events but how can we describe absolutely nothing?

We can only do so by using words that describe events and say, in this place they do not exist.

So, God is to be found in an area where there is no air, no gravity, no light but also no darkness, no thoughts, no emotions, and every type of experience that we can describe but with the word "no" in front of it.

Who amongst us can visualize such a place? And yet this place exists. It is the equivalent of zero in the arithmetical example we gave.

So, we ask you, if you can, to imagine peeling back the layers of life and experience, one by one, until absolutely nothing exists.

That zero point is the place where God is to be found.

And yet, if we are in a place where absolutely nothing exists how can God exist in that non-place?

This is the big conundrum.

God is the creator of everything and yet we could say that God cannot exist because the place where he is to be found does not exist.

We must try to answer this question if we are to progress in this essay.

We could say that if nothing exists then everything exists but it is all made of nothing!

This may or may not be true but, even if it is true, it doesn't help us much because it sounds like gobbledygook and is impossible to understand.

How can everything be made of nothing?

In the world in which we live, whether it be incarnation or in the astral realms, it is obvious that all that we can see is made of something.

None of us live in a complete nothingness.

In fact, to live in nothingness seems impossible.

For instance, if we create a perfect vacuum, we still have something we call a vacuum.

If we reduce the temperature of something to absolute zero, it can still be measured.

In neither of these two cases do we arrive at the point where the concept of air and/or temperature have no meaning.

It is quite simply that we are measuring a lack of air and/or a certain degree of coldness.

So, is it possible to imagine a place where air and heat (or lack of it) quite simply have no meaning? Even to try to imagine such a place gives meaning to that place.

After all, artists of various kinds use imagination frequently to create things: the plot of a book or film, a painting, music etc.

They start off as imagination and that is translated into a work of some kind. So, imagination is not nothing.

Perhaps all we can do is to ask you to accept zero as a point where nothing exists.

But we still have not answered the question as to why God exists in this nothingness?

Perhaps we could ask you to accept that a problem can only be resolved from a plane higher than the problem itself.

For air to exist, we ask you to accept that it was created from a plane higher than air. The only plane higher would be one where air did not exist. The same with space, time, gravity and the myriad of events that occur in life. To get to a higher plane would inevitably take us to a plane where they did not exist.

We can almost hear the brains of certain people whirring, trying to overcome these statements and we will agree that the examples we used were weak. But how can we possibly describe in any meaningful terms … nothing?

So, while we wait for the day that you experience that nothingness yourself and can then understand. We ask you to accept, if you will, that this area exists – indeed there are multiples of it – and that is the place that the prime creator lives.

And so, not to spend any more time on the centre point we wish to explore the other side.

We will just repeat, for the sake of clarity that, for those who arrive in this strange nowhere place and are able to retain control of themselves, because the first reaction on arriving at nowhere is panic. This is quite understandable of course.

Suddenly to find oneself for the first time in a place totally unknown causes the fight/flight reaction to kick in and one's first thought is to escape.

However, if one continues to visit this area we can realize that there is no danger and it is actually a very blissful experience.

So, when we get used to basking in the presence of God, some of us question if there is more.

This questioning begins to open the door, so to speak, into life on the other side of the God area.

After all, we must suppose that creation is endless and so, especially, life must continue.

So, we reach out with our mind and we learn, gradually to approach the new life rather like a ship finishing a long sea crossing and approaching a new shore.

Now, where we end up, at first, depends on us; our personality, our interests, our curiosity etc. After all the law of mutual attraction still applies – it is truly a universal law – so we are attracted to an area that is in alignment with who we are.

So, let us try to explain this alternative version of life on the other side of our life.

Strangely enough, it resembles, geographically, Earth as we know it.

The reason for this is that, when life in the 8th and 7th planes were created, the Archangels,

who also created this alternative area, used the same blueprint and thus the planet upon which we arrive looks very similar to our planet with land, seas, rivers, lakes, trees, and vegetation.

So how can we be sure that what we are observing is truly the other side of God and not us just returning to our so-called 3D realty?

As we stand and look at the landscape in front of us – using astral vision, of course – we notice slight differences. For instance, if we try to pick up a stone we find that it has no weight – or mass as it is termed. It is obvious that we are on a planet and we therefore assume that gravity applies but it is not so.

We will mention, at this point, that even in the astral realms of our reality, gravity applies and a stone would have a certain weight. The larger the stone, the heavier it would appear to us in the astral realms.

But, in this alternative version, mass has no meaning.

Therefore, we could move a mountain if we so desired.

Does this seem a familiar phrase? Did Jesus not say that we could command a mountain to move and it would?

We can tell you that the master Jesus was familiar with this alternative version of life and visited it often.

When he made that statement, he was describing to his followers what life was like on the other side of God but the rest of his lecture has been omitted from the Bible, partly because very few people then or today would be able to understand and partly because the creators of the Bible did not want people to know about this alternative life.

If people can be kept in ignorance, they are easier to control. However, the Bible occasionally reports the truth even if accidentally. So, the phrase concerning moving a mountain slipped into the Bible.

Further, if we look deeply into the stone or rock we see that it reflects our thoughts. This is difficult to describe because, here on Earth, rocks and stones appear dead.

In this alternative version of life, rocks and stones are part of us so, if we link with them with our mind, the stone links also with us and becomes, essentially, a reflection of us.

So, we can not only see ourselves in the stone but they can link with all our thoughts and emotions. In this strange, alternative reality all is truly one and so the stone and us become one.

Then, once we realize that the stone reflects us, if we look around us and use our psychic vision to project our thoughts and who we are out to the landscape, it all changes and becomes us.

It is an amazing experience to see all the landscape change and become us. It is also that we would become the landscape but as our will is stronger than the will of the landscape so our will dominates the will of the landscape and it becomes us.

Eventually, if we relax our psychic will, the landscape returns to what is was before.

So, unless we are hallucinating it is obvious that we are not in our 3D world!

Let us go on and try to present to you some more differences between our world and this strange alternative life.

You may have already noticed that we have described it as being the opposite of life as we know it here.

As all things present themselves as unique, independent life forms here in our world and as we have described one of the ways that life is the opposite in this other world, life becomes very easily one, connected life form, we would, perhaps, jump into the conclusion that everything would be the opposite to life here rather as if one was just turning things upside down.

But this is not entirely so.

Certainly, many things that have a connection to physicality are opposite – as we described with rocks – but certain things do not change.

For instance, good and evil remain the same. Love and hate remain unchanged compared to our world.

The concept of dimensions remains largely unaltered.

So, let us leave them and explore the things that do or are altered in comparison to our world.

As we explore this alternative reality we come across animals. Many resemble animals that we see on Earth. They might have different names but an elephant still looks like an elephant, a rabbit still resembles a rabbit.
However, they do not act as dumb creatures, to use this rather disrespectful phrase.

First and foremost, they would alter form as we linked with them spiritually (or psychically) rather as we described with rocks and stones.
However, as an animal is more spiritually aware than a stone, instead of the animal just being overtaken by our spiritual life force, there is a blending of the two and so we would appear to have animal characteristics, should we meet and interact with each other and the animal in question would take on some human aspects.

Not only would both of us alter physically but we would blend also our personalities and share common attributes. In fact, we would become one.
This has far reaching consequences.
For instance, here on Earth some people have studied animals and/or plants and mineral life forms and many a weighty tome has been written about them.
In this alternative reality such study is quite impossible for the simple reason that as soon as we turn our attention to something it immediately alters and takes on some of our attributes thus making it quite impossible to study in isolation.
It would only be possible to see the object; animal, vegetable, or mineral as it really is if we could subtract from our examination our own attributes leaving the object unaltered by us. This might be possible to do but, as you can imagine, is not at all easy to do.
So, for the majority of people who visit this alternative reality one must accept that everything one observes becomes blended with us and we just have to get used to that idea.
So, everything that we encounter is altered and becomes part of us and those things become part of who we are.
Thus, we wander about in a world that is always, to a greater or lesser degree, a reflection of us.

There is both night and day much as there is on Earth although one suspects that when it is day in our world it will be night there. However, even this does not have much meaning because, as planet Earth spins in relation to the sun so it is day in part of our reality and night in the other half. Although it is difficult to obtain proof in the other reality we feel that this planet also spins but in an opposite way to here on Earth.
But that is of little consequence.
We have night and day and there we have day and night.
To have night and day has some importance here on Earth and it probably has a similar importance in this other place but it is not of great consequence.

However, if we look at the sun or look into the night sky, the sun and the stars immediately react with us and blend with us so, once again, we cannot see the sun nor the stars as they really are but are observed as being altered by us.

It is worth mentioning that the moon does not exist in this alternative reality. The moon is only part of our reality.
As we have explained in other works, the moon is a natural body that has been placed in our world to reduce psychic power.
In this other world, the power of God flows in undiminished and the moon is not present – or does not appear to be present. Because everything alters as we focus on it, it is hard to know what exists and what does not. But, as far as we know, the moon does not exist in this alternate reality.
But we do think that the other planets; Mars, Mercury, Jupiter, etc, do exist much as they do in our reality.

We will also state, as we mentioned earlier that the main planet – the equivalent of planet Earth – resembles to a large degree our planet Earth but we must remember that our planet has been altered over time due to the various cataclysmic extinction level events (ELE's) that have caused land masses and seas to rise and fall. This alternative Earth remains very much as was designed by the Archangels long ago, not having been struck by any catastrophes.

Now, the burning question is, of course, is there any human type life on this planet?
The answer is yes there is and they have villages and cities as we have.

But, once again, to describe these people and their habitations is not easy due to the fact that, as soon as we concentrate on them, they blend with us and one can never be sure if we are looking at these people as they really are or as we imagine them to be.
But, we will describe as best we can what is observed but ask the reader to accept that our outlook is inevitably colored by our interpretation of what we observe.

We can say that the entire planet is inhabited much as our planet is inhabited.
There are cold areas at the poles and hot areas at the equator.

The cities and towns are built with natural materials, the people seeming to have great respect for their planet.
They are equally advanced as any group in major cities on Earth, more so in many cases as they have not been victims of ELE's that have halted progress on our Earth. However, they do not seem to chase after progress as we do and just seem to relax and enjoy life.
There are men and women and, of course, children. The procreation process appears to follow the same lines as on Earth and, generally, the children are loved and well cared for.

However, the people do not seem to eat or drink as we do, being able to draw sustenance from the astral realms much as is done in heaven.

That may be, of course, because we might be looking at their lives using our astral vision and so are not fully seeing physical beings, although life there does seem physical.
We have questioned them concerning their lives. They speak telepathically and are very friendly and open concerning their lives.

The seem to live as long as they desire, are seldom ill and have advanced medical techniques for dealing with accidents.
They do not use animals or even plants in their lives as they are able to produce suitable clothing by an act of will. They live in harmony with nature.

They seem to spend much time linking with each other, exchanging thoughts and ideas and seem always to be happy and contented.
Life in this alternative version of Earth appears to be somewhat similar to Summerland in the heavenly spheres. This is the result of living in peace with each other and with all life.
Wars and crime do not exist. There is nothing to fight over and no need to steal, rape, kill or whatever.
They are able to satisfy all their needs by telepathic and clairvoyant means and so do not need to covert other's possessions.
Their sexual impulses seem to be under control so women do not flaunt their sexuality and men do not desire them in that fashion.
When a couple bond it is because of love and a mutual blending – like attracting like.

When we blend with them we feel, intensely, their love, warmth, friendliness and compassion which supposes that we send to them our less than perfect emotions, but they do not react negatively to us. They grin and bear our presence knowing that we will eventually leave them and they can return to their former state of platonic love for all life.

They do not use money, quite simply because they have no need for it.
They have told us that they are aware of our version of planet Earth and some visit us occasionally. It somewhat dismays them that we live in such a war like fashion.

But they are aware of ascension that is affecting us positively and, by the same token, will affect them negatively.

We have already mentioned in other works this pendulum swing that bascules slowly back and forth between our two worlds bringing light to one part and darkness to the other. We will just repeat what is happening.
God's spiritual light shines on one half of this circle of life at a time.
For a long period, the light shone on them while we were in spiritual darkness, but now a change is occurring and the light is shining on us and they are moving into darkness.
Thus, we assume that, eventually, we will develop to be somewhat like them whilst they will have to undergo the living hell that we for so long experienced.

Due to the fact that they have visited us over a long period of time, they observed the darkness that we went through and are aware that they, too, must experience this.

However, for the moment at least, they are facing this dark destiny stoically, understanding the reason for it and are happy for us that we will be moving into the light.

They are preparing for the fact that they must suffer very much as we have suffered and are certainly not trying to avoid it by moving to our reality – which they could. They know that they have to go through this torment and that it is an essential part of God's means of charging his batteries, so to speak. Thus, they are facing this dismal future bravely.

So, we have presented a brief overview of this alternate world on the other side of God and we hope that it has been beneficial to you to learn about this alternate, complementary version of life.

No doubt there is much more that could be said.
No doubt, just as in our dimensions, there is a lot that we have mentioned about alternative realities, alternative universes and portals. The same exists in their reality but we have said sufficient to whet your appetite, to open the door into the wonder of God's creation.
So, we will close this overview.

ADDENDUM 3

AKASHIC RECORD

We wish to talk to you today about the way that the Akashic Record was constructed, why it was, its purpose and so on.

We wish to inform you about its connection to life, to all living things and to its vital place in the construct of life.

We have, briefly, in other works, touched on the Akashic Record and have linked it to Higher Self and have called it a living library.

But the Akashic Record is a far more complex area – or construct would be a better term – with far reaching consequences than most people could ever imagine.

The problem, as always is to know where to begin. Those of you who have followed our various discussions concerning life in general and the spiritual aspects in particular will be aware that we have gradually revealed more and more to you about the various aspects of creation and have revealed to some, information that has been unknown to the vast majority of the world's population, past or present.

Indeed, we have hesitated to give you some of the information knowing full well that it will be incomprehensible to many of you.

If we may just break off from this subject of the Akashic Record and mention the thorny subject of ET life. We have explained to you that there is life everywhere, some of it is to be found in caverns just under the surface of planet Earth, some is in astral form, yet more in interdimensional form and some of it from the alternative version of life from the other side of where prime creator is. Much of this life has visited Earth and interacted with us for long ages.

There have been countless films made in which aliens and their craft have been mentioned.

There have been many people who have seen UFO's and have had interaction with our ET cousins and yet, to this day, one still sees programs on TV, articles in journals and lectures given asking the question, "do ET's exist?"

If people are not willing to accept the evidence of ET life, what chance have we got of convincing you of the truth of all the strange things we talk about?

In fact, we do not try to convince you. We have been charged by higher beings than us humble servants of God to reveal information to you, and we leave you and future generations to accept this information as and when you are ready.

What we tell you is truth. Some of it we explain openly and some of it we couch in terms that do not state plainly the truth, because some aspects of life are so revolutionary that words do not exist to explain.

However, we never lie to you nor do we state anything unless we are sure of our facts. If some of what we tell you today seems somewhat contradictory to what we stated in the past it is quite simply that when we first started to reveal aspects of life we were aware that you could have had difficulty in understanding. So, we have prepared each essay, each book and each revelation to stand on the shoulders of previously given statements in the hopes that it will grow as you are able to accept more and more.

We are also aware that there are some who stumble on recent revelations who have not started at the beginnings of our talks and thus fail to comprehend. We have often exhorted you to start at the beginning but we cannot force you.

So, we will repeat that if what we tell you is incomprehensible to you, it is perhaps due to you not having done your homework. What we explain is wisdom laid one point after another and should make sense if you have followed our lessons one after another.

If you have skipped any lessons and do not understand what we say, we cannot be held responsible.

As a last aspect, what we have told you all so far, may well be more than has ever been revealed but we wish to say that we have only scratched the surface.

Life goes on indefinitely and we could teach for long ages and still not reveal all that there is to be revealed.

Lastly, in this section, we should say that some things are beyond even our comprehension and, thus, if we cannot understand, there is no point in trying to explain to you.

Our aim is always to explain even the most complex of topics in simple, everyday language. It has not and never will be our intention to explain topics in language incomprehensible to the general public.

Having given that introduction let us now turn our attention to explaining the Akashic Record.

The story begins in the dawns of creation when the Archangels charged with creating life, according to God's wishes, first were confronted with the seven – eight, actually – bands or carrier waves that God himself is responsible for.

As far as we are aware these carrier waves, dimensions, are the only aspect of life that we can directly attribute to God.

All else, in every aspect of life, God has placed into the hands of his trusted allies, the Archangels, the DOL that we have often mentioned.

Perhaps we should attribute the creation of these two groups of angelic beings to God also but, as we have no proof as to the origins of these beings we cannot say with any conviction that they were created by God and so we hesitate to say that they were.

Certainly, it seems to us that as nothing else other than God existed at that time, logic would dictate that they were the creation of God but, as we can neither question God nor these angelic beings as to the creator, we will not assume nor presume that it is so.

We can only state that God created the carrier waves – or dimensions – and the various servants and co-creators of God made all the rest.

Perhaps who created the Archangels and DOL is, like God himself, destined to be the one unresolved mystery.

It would be a wise man indeed – or a fool – who could claim to know where God came from. Certainly, none of us know.

But the point is, as we have often stated, into these carrier waves life was placed bit by bit.

All that is known about God is that he is light – star light – and light is vibration. It is one of the attributes of light, if it is to be used to create something, it must be flickering on and off. This type of vibration is called Alternating current. Its use is in most forms of sound and image construction. There is also another form of current called Direct current. It is a useful form of electricity but is not capable of producing sound or images directly. D.C. (as it is sometimes termed) can be used to power certain objects but, even in the case of DC creating the energy to make a light or sound producing device, the light or sound is in the form of vibration.

Thus, one of the few things we know about God is that God is light and light is AC (alternating current) and furthermore, as all life everywhere is made of God, all life must be vibrations, alternating current.

This is simple physics and, if you can accept that which the great saints have told us, which is that God is light, the rest follows on as simple fact.

Now, AC, whatever its waveform, generally, is a force which rises from a zero point to a maximum, down to a zero point again, reduces to a so called minimum and then rises to a zero point again.

We wish to state two things about what we have just described.

First, it is sometimes imagined that the rise and fall above a zero point is often described as positive and negative. This is not actually so. The rise in energy above the zero point and the opposite below zero point are just two aspects of the same force.

This is a subject that has a certain importance but, for the sake of our discussion can be considered to be two aspects of the same power.

We are describing the God force not running a course in electricity, so we will not delve deeper into this particular matter.

But, what is of paramount importance, strangely enough, is the zero point.

We hope you have studied other talks in which we stated that life is created and destroyed countless time a second.

It is because the vibration of God's life force passes by this zero point endlessly that we can say that all life is created as the power of God, passes out from zero in either direction and then it returns to zero, at which point is ceases to exist.

So, we wish you clearly to understand that life starts at a null point, rises to a node, descends to a null point, moves to another node, then returns to a null point again.

At the null point everything stops, disappears. It has to. That is the nature of AC.

It is one thing to see a waveform rising and falling on an oscilloscope but it takes a stretch of the mind to accept that same thing is happening to the entire cosmos in all dimensions, past, present, and future, but it is so. Everything, everywhere is pulsing to this beat of creation – God.

So, we need to try to link this endless pulsation to the Akashic Record.

If we can take the creative part between the two null points we can, perhaps, visualize each one as a small packet of information separated from the previous or the next packet by two null points where all disappears.

It is necessary to clearly visualize this process if one wishes to comprehend the Akashic Record so we will repeat this information.

We start with nothing at the zero or null point. Then life creates a microsecond of existence before it returns to the null point at which moment everything vanishes

Then it creates a new moment of life before stopping again.

This process has been linked to the individual frames on a cine film or endless carriages of a train each carriage linked to the next but passing before our eye endlessly.

This is happening to all things everywhere. All is one and so as one object (whatever it might be) is created and destroyed, so it is happening to all things simultaneously.

Now, it is also a fact of life that nothing created by God can ever be destroyed.

We can accept that at the null or zero points God is not creating anything, but during what we called the node moments between two null points, life is being created, not exactly by God but by his Archangels who create life with God's authorization – so things are created that are alive.

As we mentioned, once something has the authorization by God to be alive it can never die, thus each one of these frames are alive and will remain so eternally.

So, logic dictates that each frame of life should be stored somewhere.

It would be chaotic to have endless little packets of life just floating about with no attempt to put them in any order.

Therefore, each frame of life, that which we might also refer to as space/time, if either space or time really existed, are encoded with a unique stamp rather like taking a document and putting a unique mark on it so that it could be located amongst a mass of other documents.

So, difficult as this is to imagine, each separate, still frame of life is instantly encoded with a unique frequency which allow it to be stored and also located if required.

This, actually, is much more complicated than we might first imagine.

We stated, in other talks, that when the highest dimension was created, a certain, vast number of points of life were placed in this dimension. Thus, the exact number of points of life are known and each one of these points of life – without any denomination (which is to say, without knowing what their destiny in life will eventually be), nevertheless were given a unique stamp or marker.

This needs to have some explanation.

We wish you to understand that, at the very beginning of creation, God created little versions of himself – enough to fill, not only planet Earth (every grain of sand, every rock, every blade of grass, planet, insect, animal, fish and human) but also all the other dimensions and areas where anything is to be found and put a dot of life corresponding to all things into the 8th dimension and gave each dot of life a unique stamp or identity.

We are not sure if you can appreciate what we have just stated so we will labor the point somewhat.

If you can imagine, just here on Earth, all the bits and pieces of earth and rock there are, just by picking up a handful of earth and looking at the number of separate grains of earth there are in your hand, then multiply that by the size of planet Earth.

Then add to that the number of different plants there are then add to that number all the different life forms (animals and humans) there are around the planet, we think that you would arrive at a very large number indeed.

Then add to that number, the grains of earth and rock found on each planet, moon or sun throughout the galaxy, the number would increase dramatically.

Then add to all that all the beings that are to be found in all the different dimensions and inter dimensions, the number grows yet more.

Lastly, multiply that number by all life that has lived since life was first created and go on into the endless future, we think that you would agree that you would arrive at an exceedingly large number.

Well, that is the number of dots of life that God created and placed in the 8th dimension and gave each dot of life a unique identity to mark it as different from any other dot of life.

Therefore, the exact number of dots, of points, of life were, and are known, and for each of these points of life a file in a sort of giant filing cabinet – or files in a giant computer – were created in which to store each and every experience as these points of life were called into action.

Therefore, you may not know this but there is a file in this imaginary, but real, storage mechanism that exists with your identity attached to it and everything that you have experienced since creation is stored in this file. This will go on endlessly into the future and all that you have experienced, are experiencing, and will experience in the future is or will be recorded in your personal file.

The same applies to all things. Everything has a file in which its life experiences are recorded.

This is what is called the Akashic Record.

No one judges your actions. They are just recorded as they occur. This is done countless times a second.

So, just to consider you who read this essay, a vast number of files, each one uniquely encoded, are stored in your personal file in this filing cabinet – or call it a program in a computer if you prefer.

This is a sobering thought.

Nothing is hidden. Every thought, every action, every experience that you have made since the dawns of time are in your file and could be read by you or by anyone else who has the ability to enter the Akashic Record and wanted to see your file.

We have all done things of which we are not proud. We have all had bad thoughts, taken bad actions and have hurt others.

All this is stored in your file as well as all the good things that you have done.

Upon reflection, most of us would like our file to record good actions and so it might be a good idea to control our thoughts and actions so that, from now on, our file contains only good deeds. It is up to us.

The Akashic Record just records events. It is up to us to decide if these events are good or bad.

Now, what we have just described to you – every word – is true but there is another way to look at the Akashic Record. We are not sure that most of you incarnate at the moment are in a position to accept much more on this subject but we do wish to implant in your minds the concept that the Archangels who created all that we have stated did not want the Akashic Record and every one's life experiences to be too unwieldy, so they constructed an alternative way of observing life's recordings.

We will explain it in a simple fashion although we feel obliged to tell you that we are just going to create an analogy that is not really the truth concerning this alternate way of recording life's events.

We will use an example that we have stated elsewhere. From what we have just told you, we hope that you can imagine that, if we look at a car, we can realize that it is made of countless atoms, that each atom is alive and, thus, each atom has a file in the Akashic Record in which those atoms experiences are recorded.
But, when we look at a car we don't see a mass of atoms, we see a car.
Once again, we may realize that the car is just a mass of atoms which, due to people's consciousness, have been made to come together to form what we see as a car.
This vehicle may be large or small, may be designed to go at a leisurely pace or at great speed. It might be of virtually any colour and may be new or old but we call it a car.

Now here is the point that we wish to make. If we tried to count the number of atoms used to create this car, we would very soon lose track of the number of atoms but, collectively, the number that we see – a car – is one.
We see just one car.
Obviously, there are many cars but if we look at a car, we don't see an impossible to count number of atoms, each one alive, we just see one object – a car.

Now, we will not expand on that concept because it would take us into an area of spiritual physics that would be virtually impossible for most to comprehend and would be outside of the scope of this essay.
It is sufficient to say that it is possible to look into the Akashic Record and, instead of seeing an enormous amount of single frames that go to make up a person's life experience, we can see it as one collective event.
This is, of course, just as well because, if life was just presented as a mass of individually encoded frames of time/space it would be utterly incomprehensible to all of us so, the Archangels cleverly connected a person's life experiences and encoded all that so that we see one event.
Now, we could use the example of a film that consists of many single frames, each one following on one after another in a stream of sound and image that shows us a film.
But to watch all the film, we would need to let the projector roll on from the beginning to the end of the film.
In the Akashic Record, we can see an event as one piece of time/space. An event, no matter how long it may have lasted in 3D reality – an incarnation for example – can be assimilated in a microsecond.

This is a very valuable way of watching events in the Akashic Record and also very valuable to those who wish to learn.
For instance, if we located the life of an excellent scientist who created many things that other people have hidden from us, not only could we watch the scientist's experiments but could see everything that he did in a flash of time. We would not need to watch him struggling to solve problems in real time. We could appreciate the struggle and find the conclusion in no time at all.

Now, we have mentioned this and, if ever you visit the Akashic Record, you can make use of this phenomenon but we do, generally, like to explain the logic behind our statements. In this case, however, the technique used to join vast numbers of images into one, instant download of information is, as we said, outside of this discussion. Therefore, we will just say that, if you visit the Akashic Record you will be able, instantly, to download the information you are seeking into your mind and then into your brain.

Now we must try to answer some questions that may arrive.
First, where is the Akashic Record?
The answer is that it is in the 5th dimension. It is connected on one side, if we may thus explain it, to higher self and on the other side to imagination in the 6th dimension. We have explained this in great detail in the book Auras.
What is the speed that life is created and destroyed?
A moment in time has been calculated to be 1×10 to the negative 43 seconds, which is a very short moment in time. This is not exactly true but we do not wish to give the exact time because it could be used by evil people to destroy life. So, we will not give the exact frequency.

We hope that this brief and incomplete overview of the Akashic Record has been helpful to you. The Akashic Record is a very important part of life and we look forward to the day when all good people can enter it and learn.

Printed in Great Britain
by Amazon

80519158R00066